Forewor

This is a true story - long overdue
Personal memories of Walter by John Coles

I was born in January 1944 just five months before D Day 6th June 1944. My earliest memories was the very cold Winter of 1947, when snow and freezing conditions over the British Islands were really bad. In 1947 we were living in the county of Dorset as my father was a farmer and he was in charge of the farm workers, including 47 German Prisoners Of War. He got on well with them as they all worked well on the land. Not one tried to escape. They all lived in wooden huts which were kept warm and all were fed well.

My mother gave birth to four boys and I was the second born. To most people after the war, life was very hard, as food was on ration, even bread, as we were sending bread into Germany to feed the people there. During the war bread was not on ration in Britain. Looking back on those times I consider we were lucky as my father, being a farmer, used to come home with fresh milk which was still warm from the cows. Also he came home with butter, cheese, and cream. We also had plenty of vegetables, including turnips, cabbage and swedes. There was also plenty of rabbits to eat.

Walter Schnitzer was one of those 47 German POW on our farm. Sometimes Walter was allowed into our home on the farm and I can remember my mother knitting a pair of woollen gloves and socks for him. I can also recall Walter chasing after a rabbit in a field and catching it and into the pot it went! Walter was a very big man - strong as and Ox, with very large hands. He could make and do with anything. As one of four small boys he used to make us wooden toys, when he wasn't working into the fields.

In 1946 a young boy fell into a very deep well on a nearby farm. News soon spread about the boy and Walter ran over to the farm to see everyone just standing around the well, making no attempt to rescue the lad. Walter found a rope and let himself down into the well which was twenty five feet deep with little water at the bottom. He tied the rope around the boy and he was hauled up. Then the rope was lowered again so that Walter could get out. On getting out of the well, Walter blacked out as there was no air at the bottom of the well. When he came round in fresh air, a farmer pulled out a gun and pointed it at Walter's head. "Are you going to shoot me then?" Walter said. The farmer said to him "What is a German doing with an English boy?" A farmhand knocked the gun out of the farmer's hand. Sadly the boy died. Walter said afterwards if someone had gone down the well sooner he could have been saved.

In the Summer of 1948 Walter received his De-mob papers and went home to Germany, where he went to see his father and other family members. His father was never very nice to him, even as a small boy. After six months in Germany looking for work and in Walter's own words "the whole of Germany was in a mess!", he decided to come back to Dorset in England. That was the very last time he saw his father. Walter decided to come back to the same farm where my father was. My father found him an old caravan and they both patched it up. That is where he lived for a while. He was paid one pound and ten shillings a week. (One pound and fifty pence in today's money). On pay day Walter used to come to our house with a mars bar each for myself and my three brothers and two bottles of fizzy pop 'Tizer' and my mother would give him a hot meal. In 1949 our baby sister was born. In total that was now a family of five children. In late 1949 my father decided to move from Dorset and took a job farming at the village of Street in Somerset where C&J Clarks, the well known shoe factory was based. Walter came with us and lived in the family home i.e. the Coles family. So it was goodbye Dorset. I am still very fond of that county and in the Summer months we drive down along the coast - sometimes stopping to do some sea fishing from the beach with my wife Sandra.

It is interesting that my late father-in-law fought at the battle of Monty Cassino, as Walter had done in his Stuka dive bomber. This battle was very hard and lasted for five months, in 1944. It was also known as the Battle for Rome. In 1951 Walter first met Hildegard in Street. At first she did not like Walter, but soon warmed to him and only six months later after their first meeting they were married at St Mary's Catholic Church in Glastonbury, some two miles from Street. My mother spruced us all up and we all attended the Wedding. Hildegard was 23 years old at the time and Walter was 27. At the time Hildegard was working at Weston-Super-Mare General Hospital as a nurse and every day Walter got on his old bicycle to see her at Weston and then bicycled back home again to Street - a distance of 44 miles! He was only allowed to see her for half an hour as she had to get back to her hospital ward.

Two local children sitting on Walter's motorbike in 1960

After they were married they rented a small cottage in Street in an area called 'The Mead'. By this time my father gave up farming and got a job in Glastonbury as a long-distance lorry driver, as it was much better paid. Walter too left farming and was employed at C&J Clarks and stayed there for just over forty years.

In the Summer of 1952 Walter helped a local farmer just outside Glastonbury with hay-making. He decided to make it the biggest hayrick in Somerset. And he did! It even got into the local paper.

*The farm workers and the huge hayrick.
Walter is standing on the far right*

During the war, Hildegard was fighting fires after the bombing raids over Germany. She was only fourteen years old.....When the war came to an end food became very scarce and her mother told her to see if she could find food anywhere. She had an old bicycle and some sack bags tied to the handlebars. So off she went and cycled miles and miles to see what she could find. She was still very young, so for her own safety she made herself as unobtrusive as possible, as at that time many women were raped.

She was gone from home for over a week and slept in old buildings and barns which were bomb-damaged. She found potatoes and vegetables but no meat. She also found a lot of dead bodies on the roadside. Luckily she got home safely. It was not safe for a woman to travel at night because of the many rapes that were being committed.

In 1966 their Son, Julian was born. Hildegard was advised not to have any more children as she had suffered a very bad back injury as a young woman. When she found out that she was expecting a baby she was told by her doctor that she had to stay in bed until the birth. After the baby was born she was told not to have any more. At the time they were living at a very nice caravan park and made many friends in the village of Pedwell, six miles from Street. Sometime in the late sixties they moved into a farm cottage just across the road from the caravan park, which they rented.

In 1969 my twin daughters were born. When they were about 8 years old Hildegard invited us down for a meal. We lived close by in Glastonbury. She was a very good cook. My daughters often talk about Hilda's lovely cakes and jelly they had for afters.

Walter had a thing about speed. He bought a big 650cc motorbike and could often be seen doing 90 miles an hour going through Street high street. He used to go so fast you couldn't read his number plate! Later on he got himself a car, which he drove to Germany every year. Walter outlived most of his family members. In 1957 another sister was born, now making a family of six children. By then I was looking forward to leaving school, which I did in 1959.

Walter did not like old age. He had to give up driving as he had a blackout and ended up hitting a tree. He then got himself a top of the range mobile scooter with a top speed of 35 miles an hour. He often came to see us at our home in Glastonbury from Street on his scooter. By this time Walter and Hildegard had bought a house at Willow Road in Street. Walter was now over 90 years old and finding it difficult to walk. He took several falls. It was decided Walter needed to be put into a care home. He was there for four months.

Just before he passed away my brother Roy and I went to see him. It was a nice sunny day and we took him out into the sunshine in his wheelchair and had a nice long chat. Walter said to us that he did not like this place as it was full of old people who seemed to be asleep all the time.

Rest in Peace Walter. We all miss you.
Foreword by John Coles, former Mayor of Glastonbury

P.S. Walter never got a speeding ticket.....as he was going too fast to read the number plate

Walter Schnitzer 15 November 1924 to 2 November 2015

Walter & Hildegard

The incredible story of two survivors

Introduction

Walter is one our local characters. We often see him out and about, nowadays on his electric powered 'buggy'. You can't miss him wearing, as he always does, his Bavarian hat and traditional green woollen overcoat. Walter is larger than life in many ways. He seems to know just about everyone he meets and local people often stop for a chat with him. Walter likes to tell people about adventures during his long life. He's in his eighties now and has a quite story to tell; some would say he has led a charmed life. Walter's life , spanning as it does the years leading up to WWII through to the present, has been truly amazing; sometimes tragic at other times miraculous and yet optimism always shines through. This life story is so special that I thought it should be recorded. Although Walter lives in England and therefore speaks English most of the time his mother tongue is German. So I offered to help him write his story. We sat together while he talked and I took notes and asked questions. I have changed nothing and added only a few historical footnotes to put his stories into context. What follows is Walter's story in his own words.

Robert Steele 2010

Walter Schnitzer

A record of a converstion by Robert Steele

I am pleased and honoured that Walter's family has invited me to say a few words about Walter, a local character who many of us have known maybe in his place of work or as a neighbour or just seeing him whizzing by on his buggy proudly wearing his Bavarian hat. Walter had a long, colourful and, many would say charmed, life which he lived to the full. Indeed a life in which he narrowly escaped death on several occasions. He also struck me as a very contented man with a generous nature who had an accepting attitude towards all that happened to him during his long life. He always enjoyed talking about his experiences and I decided some time ago that I must record these stories so that others can continue to learn about his life and times. I'll give you just a little taste of Walter's story now.

When Walter was telling me one of his stories he said to me: "I don't consider myself to be special or important. I'm an ordinary bloke. I was born into a working class family in Bavaria and most of my life I've been an ordinary working man. But some extraordinary things have happened to me from the moment I was born. I've led a charmed life I reckon living through some remarkable times and life threatening adventures in my long life and I consider myself lucky to be alive to tell the tale. I have never let anything get me down. I'm always optimistic and although I've never shied away from danger or hard work and never been afraid to take risks in my life yet I have always had a very strong sense of self preservation. I've been very lucky and mostly very happy and certainly content all my life. I'm an old man now but I have never lost the spirit which has always driven me. "

Walter was born between the two world wars on 15 November 1924 in Bad Tölz in Upper Bavaria, Germany not far from Munich. Bad Tölz is a lovely little town in a very pleasant part of Bavaria very near to the mountains.

Walter continued .... I had quite an unhappy childhood. I was born with crooked legs and my father couldn't bear this. I had several operations on my legs until at last they were straight enough for me to start to learn to walk. I was seven years old by that time and started school. There I must have learned how to read and write but I can't remember much about all that. I do remember once I took a catapult into class and shot something at the teacher. The other boys had dared me to do it and I have a habit of rising to a challenge. I must have been a good shot because I hit the teacher- but he never discovered who had done it! I was always a bit of a rebel.

Life at home was hard for me and by the time I was nine or ten I had run away from home at least four times but when I was fourteen and had left school I went out to work in the nearby plywood factory. My mother died in the Spring of 1940 when I was fifteen. I had no mother to care for me and a father that loathed me. Things were not looking good for me. To add to this the whole country was in a kind of madness because Hitler was now in power and everything seemed to be changing. My life was in turmoil so I decided, just before my sixteenth birthday, to run away for good. I took my bicycle. I had no bag of possessions or food and no money with me. I didn't even have a map. I set off north cycling towards Wolfenbuttel where my step brother lived, about 400 miles from Bad Tölz. It was quite an adventure. Each night I slept rough wherever I could and as soon as it became light each day I got back on my bicycle and continued heading north, eating apples I found on the way. When I arrived I was welcomed in. It was a strange feeling to be in a house and felt at ease.

I got a job at the local Fokker aeroplane factory at Bussing. The factory was manufacturing Fokker Wolf fighter planes at the time and I was put to work on the engine manufacturing line. This was completely different work from what I was used to but I soon adapted to it. I enjoyed my work at the Fokker factory and it seemed natural to me that I should learn to fly planes since I knew quite a bit about how they were built. So I took the opportunity offered to me to join the German equivalent of the Air Cadets and had free flying lessons near the factory every Sunday. I really enjoyed this and really wanted to be a flyer. By the time I was seventeen and a half I had earned my pilot's licence. For me learning to fly was a great new opportunity for a daredevil like me to have more adventures.

Soon after gaining my pilot's licence I was 'called up'. I was conscripted into the Luftwaffe as a pilot with the rank 'Gefleiter' with one stripe on my arm. I was posted to Bussing, an air base near Braunsweig, and received six month's intensive training flying Junkers 87 'Stuka' dive bombers. Stukas were not every pilot's favourite aeroplane by any means. They were old fashioned and not easy to handle. What's more pilots thought of them as death traps. What they were good at was dive bombing enemy targets with sirens blaring for which they had gained a terrifying reputation. I didn't mind flying them at all. I wasn't the sort to be scared, I just got on with the job.

Flying was good and in 1942, when I was eighteen, I was

13

posted to the Russian front near Stalingrad. Stukas were used in many battle dive bombing scenarios but at Stalingrad we were dive bombing Russian tanks. Flying low over the area I was able to see the battle going on below me. It was really cold when winter arrived. We lived in really harsh conditions with hardly any heat and no comforts at all. Every morning, when we were woken up by the sergeant, we were made to strip naked and go outside in the freezing cold for morning exercises, including running bare foot in the deep snow and ice - I was told it was 40 degrees below freezing some days. These exercises were intended to toughen us up for fighting in these incredibly harsh conditions and to be ready to face the ferocious Russian enemy.

A Stuka had two seats, one behind the other. As the pilot I sat in front and Hans, my machine gunner, behind me. On one of my sorties my plane was hit by Russian anti aircraft fire. I started to go down but I managed to bring the aircraft around and very fortunately for me managed to crash land and even more fortunately for me the crash landing was behind the German lines. We had been warned in our training that for German airmen to be captured by Russians meant certain death so I didn't bail out using the ejector seat and parachute. My plane ended up with its nose buried in the ground and was wrecked but both of us got out alive and managed to escape with only comparatively minor injuries. After a few weeks I was posted to Monte Cassino in Italy where there was fierce fighting against the Allies. Not long after arriving there and carrying out bombing sorties I got shot down again and another of my planes was wrecked. Once again I managed to crash-land behind German lines. Not long afterwards I was posted back to Stalingrad. Again I crash-landed and tragically my fellow airman was killed. I was badly injured and, as always in these situations, there is a big risk that the aircraft will catch fire or explode so I needed to get away. When I got out of the wreckage, I worked out my location from the maps with me. I found myself to be about 6 km behind Russian lines. I'm not easily frightened by anything but this was a very dangerous situation for me. If I was found by the Russians I would be shot for sure. I decided to hide during the day and move at night. I was badly injured with bullet wounds in my shoulder and the side of my body and I was losing a lot of blood. I had no supplies of food or water. When I think back on that time it makes me shudder. Moving was extremely painful for me and I could only move a very short distance at a time but somehow I managed to crawl, painfully slowly, on my elbows and knees. After a night of this I was totally done in and it was as much as I could do to crawl into a hole in the snow and keep still and hopefully sleep for a while until it was dark again. I don't know how but I managed to keep this up for four long nights. By that time I had lost so much blood that I was as weak as a kitten and frozen to the marrow. The only drink available was the snow and there was plenty of that around fortunately. At the end of the fourth night of crawling I eventually reached the German lines. Imagine my relief to see German uniforms and friendly faces.

The war was not going well for Germany and petrol was in very short supply. There was not enough fuel for the few remaining air-worthy aircraft left after the allied attacks on our tanker fleet. Because of this all of us ended up being transferred to the Wehrmacht (Germany army). My flying days were at an end.

So now I was in the Wehrmacht, and a soldier. My army unit consisted of 120 men. We received just two week's army basic training and each of us was issued with a bicycle as there was no fuel for army vehicles. We didn't even have enough proper weapons or ammunition; it was all rather sad and pathetic and not at all like we had imagined the army to be like. We were taken by train to Holland near Eindhoven. My unit was sent off to fight but due to my injuries my orders were to guard the bikes. While I was waiting there, guarding all those bikes, for what seemed ages a friendly Dutchman came up to me and offered to give me some food. He was quite chatty and spoke a little German and told me that he was interested in the bicycles, which were all fairly new and in quite good condition. He offered to pay me for them. He went on to tell me about the terrible battle which had wiped out the German soldiers and that the British were only about one mile away from where we were standing. From what he had just said to me it was clear that probably none of my unit was going to come back for me or their bikes. He asked me what I was going to do. I decided that the only sensible course of action was to give myself up as a POW. After all it wouldn't look good to be charged with a black market offence either by my own officers or as a POW by the Allies. I was arrested by two soldiers dressed in full Scottish regalia and taken to their camp. I don't know what happened to the bikes but I do know that from that moment my war was over - I was a POW. Later, in the compound, I met my unit captain and two other soldiers from the unit. They looked in a bad way and I found out from them that of the 120 men in my unit who left me looking after the bikes only those three had survived the battle. The unit had been virtually wiped out by Allied fire - I had been very lucky once again !

After my surrender to the British I was eventually taken to England. I ended up in a POW camp near Shaftesbury. We lived in the camp at night and during the day we were taken out to local farms for forced labour. One job I had was feeding 500 pigs. In the mornings I used to go with the farmer in his lorry to the camp and other places to get swill to feed the pigs. Once, I remember, the farmer took out his handkerchief from his pocket to blow his nose and a revolver fell out on to the floor. I spotted this of course. The farmer was very edgy and quite obviously embarrassed. I could speak a bit of English by that time so I said to him "You don't need that gun to protect yourself from me - if I had wanted to kill you I would have done it a long time ago." He got the message and laughed. We got on really well from that day on. I was there for about 6 months. I didn't feel like a prisoner really and became quite content living and working out in the countryside.

While I was working at a farm the farmer's wife from the neighbouring farm came running up to me in a real state. She was gasping and hardly able to speak but managed to get me to understand that she wanted me to come quickly because her son had an accident. In fact he had fallen down the well at their farm. It never occurred to me as in any way odd that she asked me, a German POW, rather than anyone else for help. Of course I went with her straight away. When I arrived there were about half a dozen men staring hopelessly down the well shaft but none of them would go down. They were saying that it was too dangerous to go down, that you could drown or die of suffocation and that the bloke had probably drowned down there already. I couldn't understand why nobody was trying to save him. I didn't hang about. I pushed the other blokes aside and got right up to the top of the well. I grabbed the rope they had and told them to hang on to the end. I then started going down the ladder: When I had gone down about

20 feet I noticed that it was hard to breathe, there was very little air down there. I kept going down and eventually reached the man at the bottom. It was pitch dark and wet and my lungs were gasping for air. I could see that the man's head wasn't completely underwater but he wasn't moving either. We got him out but by the time the doctor arrived the farmer's son was pronounced dead. I never once thought of him as one of the enemy, he was another human being and I felt the same sorrow as if he'd been a fellow German. I also thought how lucky I was to have survived after that experience down there with hardly any air to breathe. In fact of all the close shaves I've had in my life, and there have been quite a few as you know, that was probably the nearest I came to death myself.

After many adventures I moved from Dorset to Street in Somerset, with David 'Dai' Coles family. We went to a farm in Cranhill Road. There's no farm there these days. While I was there a friend of the Coles family told me about a young German woman called Hildegard he knew about who lived nearby. He must have been a bit of a match-maker come to think of it, trying to bring the German boy and girl together! Anyway I was at the cinema in Street with my German friend who worked in Meare one day and I told him about Hildegard. When I met her we talked away for quite some time. I found out that she came from Bavaria like me. She said that she had come to England to learn to speak English. The rest is history as they say. We decided to get married -the wedding was in this church. Later, when we lived at Pedwell, our son Julian was born. After my farming days, I got a job at the Avalon Leather board factory in Street, part of Clarks, where I worked until I retired .

This is just a taster of the many stories that Walter told me. I could tell you about his love of speed on his motor bikes and his fast Audi cars. Or I could tell you about his amazing work ethic which impressed many fellow workers at Clarks and much more. I could also tell you about his enthusiasm for shopping and his daily visits to Lidl where he would stock up with all sorts of goodies which, because of his generous nature, he would then give to friends and neighbours. Not to mention his love of gathering walnuts, apples and blackberries which he also gave away to others.

I consider myself fortunate to have been befriended by such a lovely man - one of life's genuine characters who lived life to the full and to a great age in spite of all the odds and I believe he has left this world a better place just for having been among us.

Rest in peace Walter

Part One

Walter

My name is Walter Schnitzer. I don't consider myself to be special or important. I'm an ordinary bloke and have never wanted to be famous or rich and I'm certainly not. I was born into a working class family in Bavaria and most of my life I've been an ordinary working man living for the last 60 years or so in an ordinary house in a quiet little town in the west of England. But some extraordinary things have happened to me from the moment I was born. These things have shaped my life and made me the man I am today. A pattern of extraordinary things happening to me seems to have become part of my way of life. I've led a charmed life I reckon. I've lived through some remarkable events and life threatening adventures in my long life and I consider myself lucky to be alive to tell the tale. I have never let anything get me down. I'm always positive and optimistic. And although I've never shied away from danger or hard work and never been afraid to take risks in my life, I have always had a very strong sense of self preservation. It's just as well or I wouldn't be here to tell my story now. I've been very lucky and mostly very happy and certainly content all my life. I'm an old man now but I have never lost the spirit which has always driven me. I hope you find my story interesting and maybe inspiring but I don't tell my story for you to think how wonderful I am. I tell it because these things really happened and I don't want the memories I have to be lost or forgotten.

Walter Schnitzel 2010

Chapter 1
My early life

I was born between the two world wars on 15 November 1924 in Bad Tölz in Upper Bavaria, Germany about 30 miles south of Munich Germany's second largest city. Bad Tölz is a very lovely little town in a very pleasant part of Bavaria very near to the mountains. Nowadays it's popular with tourists and Hildegard and I still like to visit and make the effort, even at our advanced age, to travel there every year. Bavaria is part of Germany of course but life there is different to life in northern Germany. Both the whole atmosphere you get in the area and the nature of the people are quite different to what you find in Berlin and that northern part of the country. I think it's much more beautiful and friendly. Bavaria borders with Austria and in many ways we Bavarians are more like Austrians than Germans. People are different, more gentle and friendly and we are very conservative and the Catholic Church is still very strong there. The pace of life is a bit slower down there and we even speak more slowly with a kind of sing-song accent. Many people still wear tradition Bavarian costume, some every day (actually I still do even though I live in Somerset!). We have time for people and when we meet we don't use the north German greeting of 'Guten Tag' (good day) we say 'Gross Gott' (God's greeting or God be with you). We know how to enjoy ourselves too, the best beer in the world comes from Munich! I grew up with these people in this Bavarian environment.

Bad Tölz used to be called Tölz but in the middle of the

19th century people discovered natural springs. The town began to focus on the healing properties of the iron-rich springs, and became a Kur Stadt (cure and spa town) and in 1899 it became known as Bad Tölz. The town is also known

Bad Tölz Upper Bavaria

for its medieval old town, spectacular views of the Alps and as a pilgrimage site. On November 6th there is a festival to Saint Leonard of Noblac. In 1718 a chapel was built in his honour on the Calvary hill. Another major attraction is Stadtpfarrkirche, a church built in 1466 which is an excellent example of German late-Gothic architecture so I'm told.

Bad Tölz is the principal town in the district of Bad Tölz-Wolfratshausen, which is one of the alpine districts on the German-Austrian border. The valley of the Upper lsar River separates the Bavarian Alps from the Austrian Alps.

The highest peak of the district is the Schafreuter (2100 m). Bad Tölz sits on the Isar River, 700 metres above sea level. There has been a settlement there for hundreds of years and I'm reliably informed that in the 14th century Tölz became a crossroads for the salt and lumber traffic on the River Isar.

There is a military training academy there too and in 1937 it became a SS- Junkerschule (SS Officer Candidate School) which operated until the end of World War II in 1945. Also a subcamp of the Dachau concentration camp was located in the town (there's a memorial to the victims in the main street in the town). The labour camp provided labour for the SS - Junkerschule and the Zentralbauleitung (Central Administration Building). Much later, after WWII, the former SS Junkerschule became the base of the U.S. Army's 1st Battalion, 10th Special Forces Group until 1991. Bad Tölz has a population of about twenty thousand people. People work in the local industries and factories including one for making plywood and also lots of hotels and guest houses for tourists especially on the other side of the River Isar. Many people are very religious and there are several Catholic churches. The one in the main street has a large onion tower which is typical in Bavarian churches. I was supposed to go to church every Sunday but I usually stayed outside as I was not really interested in church.

My parents were Fritz and Johanna (Hanni) Schnitzer. Fritz was a short man, a head shorter than me and balding but always quite smartly dressed. I have very few pleasant memories of him except that he played the zither and sang Bavarian folk songs as many people have traditionally done down the ages in that part of Germany. He never included me in any musical fun times though. Fritz was my mother's second husband and a few years younger than her. My real father, my mother's first husband, was killed in World War I but I have no memories of him. My mother was a tall, good looking woman with a kind, if rather well worn, face. Hanni was a good mother and a resourceful wife who could turn her hand to most practical things. That was the way most families managed in those days. How things have changed nowadays. I remember watching her working away at needlework or cooking and thinking what clever hands she had. She was a skilful seamstress, for instance, and made clothes for the whole family and also clothes to sell to neighbours. Well like many families we could always make use of the extra money. Like many women at that time she could turn her hand to most things - people were more skilful in those days I think and certainly less dependent on shop goods. It was very hard times for us in Germany between the wars, probably even more so than in England. Our economy was in a really bad state. Hanni was always kind to me. I remember her warm smiles and the feel of her arms all around me comforting me and she was like this with all seven of us children. I admired her and I loved her. I certainly can't say the same about my father. There was certainly no love between us- quite the opposite in fact.

I was born a cripple. My legs were deformed and bent out of shape. I don't know what medical experts would call my condition but whatever it was I was the only one in the family born like that and it must have been a shock to everyone to have such a child to care for. My father could not bear me. He just could not face having a cripple for a son. From the moment I was born until the day he died he could not bear to be near me. Our relationship went from bad to worse. He never said a kind word to me or about me; I think he hated me so I never knew the love of a father. He never sat near me or talked to me except with angry words. He used to call me 'the cripple' and humiliate me whenever he could. His outbursts of uncontrollable anger, which often led to me being beaten by him over trivial things, are among my earliest memories and went on all the time I lived under his roof. I could tell you about so many incidents of things that he did to me which showed how much he hated me. One of these still haunts me to this day and I often have bad dreams about it. I remember, as a small child, I cried out in my sleep and for some reason it was he who came up stairs to see me not my mother. Instead of comforting me, as my mother or any normal father would have done, he shouted at me to shut up and hit me around my face. Punishing me just for dreaming. I was terrified of him and I hated him. It was not in my nature to be able to accept this sort of treatment and just put up with it. I have always had a lot of spirit and a strong sense of what's right and what's wrong. I realise now that, as I grew older, a tremendous resentment was growing in me and I eventually knew for sure that one day all that hatred and frustration would surely come bursting out in some spectacular way. In my childish mind I desperately wanted to punish him for making my life a misery. I needed to get even with him.

My condition as a cripple was carefully monitored by doctors in the town and when I was about nine months old the specialist medics started what turned out to be an incredibly long process in order to straighten out my legs. To do this it was necessary to firstly break my leg bones in several places and then re-set the bones in different positions. But it couldn't be done in one operation because my condition was too severe and also because my bones were growing all the time of course. In fact the process of breaking my leg bones and resetting them was repeated four times over the years until at last my legs were straight enough for me to start to learn to walk. I was seven years old by that time. When I think back on those times when I was so young I find it hard to imagine all the pain and distress I had to endure. Not only during the actual surgery in hospital but afterwards because my legs had to be encased in plaster all the time during my early childhood. It was my stepbrother, Sepp, who used to take me on the train to Munich for this treatment. I remember he used to carry me in his strong arms or sometimes I'd have a pick-a-back along the streets and up and down steps. My father never went with me. He was not interested in me or my treatment and he was too busy anyway. He was a carpenter who worked for a furniture manufacturing company in our town. He wanted nothing to do with me. My mother was too busy working as a post delivery women working from 7am until noon each day to help make ends meet. Then she had the running of our household so she had no time for taking me all the way to Munich and staying there during the weeks of my treatment. So Sepp became like a substitute father to me in a way and we built up quite a close relationship even though he was only my step brother. It was to him that I turned if my mother wasn't around and I needed support. I could talk things through with him and share my thoughts knowing he would take up my cause if necessary. He was well aware of the way my father treated me and often spoke up in my defence. Of course Sepp was not my father's real son so there was no great bond between them anyway. Nevertheless Sepp had to be careful about what he did and said as he needed a roof over his head so he couldn't do very much to help me. Because of all this medical treatment and therapy it wasn't until after I was seven that I eventually learned how to walk. I didn't learn to walk like other young children do of course. I had to be taught to do this. It was a long, painful process and I was very unsteady on my feet for a very long time. Walking was very hard for me - but I was, and still am, by nature very determined and eventually I managed to walk unaided. Being able to walk meant that at long last I could start school and begin to live a more normal life like other children. Until then the only teaching I had received was from my mother and that was precious little as she was so busy. It was a tremendous feeling of release from captivity into freedom as I walked my way from the home which had so many bad memories for me, to the school where new opportunities and friendships awaited me. It's hard to convey to you just how wonderfully free and empowered I felt at that moment. Not that school was a bed of roses for children in those days, teachers were very strict. More about that later.

At the end of school each day I had to come home of course and just had to make the best of it. There were seven children living in our house: Hanni, my step sister was born in 1914 so she was ten years older than me and she didn't really have much interest in her little cripple stepbrother. Then there was Sepp, my stepbrother who was born in 1915. Although nine years my senior he and I got on well and he had a very caring way with me. Then there were the twins Fritz and Rosa born in 1922. Even though they were my siblings I can hardly remember much about them so I guess we never really had much of a relationship. However I did have a close relationship with my brother Eduard. He was always known as Eddi and was born in 1925 so just a little younger than me. Eddi and I kept in touch all our lives. Last of all there was little Otto who was born in 1934. I got on fairly well with him too. I kept in touch with Eddi and Otto until they died a few years ago. All my family from those days are dead now, the only link I have is with Eddi's wife and some nieces and nephews.

We lived on the edge of town in a three bedroom semi-detached house - what in England would be called a council house. It was nothing special apart from having an enormous shed which we called the barn. The house is still there to this day and looks just the same as I remember it as a child except that the barn, which was round the back of the house, is gone now. My mother and father had one bedroom and there was another for the boys and the third for the girls. I remember that we boys slept in bunk beds. Down stairs there was a living room and a kitchen with a cooker like a kitchen range that burned wood and coal. We ate quite well, mostly simple but quite nutritious food. My mother was a good cook and we never went hungry even though money was tight in Germany in those inter-war years. We had traditional heavy Bavarian furniture in our house all of which my father had made himself. He was a skilled carpenter and made the chairs and tables, the sitting room furniture and even the enormous open fronted cupboard that we called the schrank where my mother proudly displayed her best china plates and ornaments including decorated bier steiner. To be fair to my father he was good at his craft and all the furniture was of excellent quality and extremely sturdy; but as you'll find out later, not quite sturdy enough.

We ate traditional Bavarian meals such as heavy, dark pumpernickel bread with jam or cheese and coffee for breakfast. For lunch or dinner we had meat, usually pork or rabbit with potatoes, peas and dumplings. To be fair to my father he was a good provider so none of us went hungry in our household. Like many families in those days we did have a radio in the house but I don't remember listening to it much. My father used to insist that we were quiet during important news broadcasts. I usually got sent upstairs or out to the barn. I can't remember ever having any toys or playing games with my brothers or sisters. When I was a cripple I couldn't join in with much and afterwards I was just too busy because my father made sure I earned my keep and ensured that my only hobby was the work he forced me to do for him.

We all wore traditional Bavarian clothes. Everyone did in those days - actually many people still do to this day. I still wear traditional Bavarian clothing myself even though I live in England, and I'm told that I'm known for it. We boys always wore lederhosen, which are leather trousers with patterned braces and a chest strap.

Lederhosen are virtually indestructible as they are made from leather and seem to stretch so they grow with you as you get older - a great advantage as there was no need to continually buy bigger ones or replace trousers made of fabric which could tear. For most of the year we went barefoot, shoes were an expensive item and growing feet meant bigger sized shoes all the time so even more expense. Only on Sundays and in the winter did my father let us wear our hand-me-down shoes. Believe me winters in Bavaria are cold and there's plenty of ice and snow from November until March at least, after all Bad Tölz is on the edge of The Alps. Outside our house there was not much land so we didn't have a big garden but we had a big shed - our barn. In the barn my father kept his animals. We had two pigs, two goats, a dozen hens and over two hundred rabbits in wire hutches. The animals were an important part of how our family made ends meet. We weren't the only family like this. Many people kept animals for food and to sell to others to supplement their income; times were hard.

Once I was able to walk, my father chose me to look after the animals. I wasn't given any choice in this matter and none of my brothers or sisters were made to help me - it was my job whether I liked it or not. Actually it wasn't all bad. At least I was out of the house and away from my father unless he came out checking up on me. One of the tasks I had was to go off on my old wreck of a bike to collect swill for the pigs from local hotels of which there were quite a few in the posh part of town. I had to balance the swill cans on the handlebars. It was a bit like riding a stunt bike in a circus and took quite a lot of skill to stay upright and I didn't always succeed. Many is the time I had to pick myself up off the road covered in pig swill. I fed the hens too. But the hardest job of all was collecting grass to feed the goats and rabbits. I went off on my bike all around the lanes in the area with large bags on my handlebars and cut the long grass from the road sides. It was a back-breaking and massive task for me every day. It took many bike loads to gather enough grass to feed so many animals. In fact this job took me so long after I had returned home from school each day that I had no time to do my homework. I was just so dog-tired that I fell into my bunk bed completely exhausted.

School starts at 8am in Germany so I had no time to do school work before school started. So I was in trouble at school every day for not doing my homework and just about every day

I was caned on my hands or my backside - usually six times. It became part of my everyday routine - "Bend over Schnitzer". It was useless to explain the problem that I had to the teachers. They wouldn't have listened and even if they had and then contacted my father that would have made him hate me even more, if that was possible, and he certainly would have hit me for causing him trouble from the school teachers. My school was for boys aged six to fourteen; all the teachers were men. Despite the canings I actually quite liked school and found I had no trouble learning all my lessons. Being at school was like being in a completely different world, an escape from all the hateful things I had to endure at home. For a start my father wasn't there so I had a break from him. There were friends there to lark about with and teachers to play tricks on. I was good at that! I remember some of my school lessons. A friend at school taught me how to play the zither. A zither is a traditional stringed instrument used a lot in Bavarian folk music. You play it sitting at a table usually and you have to pluck the stings with the fingers of one hand while stopping the strings for different notes with the fingers of the other hand. Somehow my father found out that I could play the zither a bit. You might think, because he was also an accomplished zither player, that he would be pleased and perhaps suggest that we could play our zithers together. But no, he was really angry with me and beat me. Perhaps he saw me as a threat to his musical talent or more likely he just really hated me and this was another excuse to give me a hard time. Back in school I remember some history lessons. We were taught about German history of course: Hermann, Frederick the Great, German unification under Bismark, the Deutscher Reich, Kaiser Wilhelm and so on. I remember some geography lessons too so I learned where the main towns in

Germany were although we Bavarians didn't really feel the need to know much about anywhere outside Bavaria. We naturally had other lessons. After all I must have learned how to read and write but I can't remember much about all that. I do remember once I took a catapult into class and fired a dried pea or something at the teacher. The other boys had dared me to do it and I have a habit of rising to a challenge. I must have been a good shot because it hit him - but he never discovered who had done it! I was always a bit of a rebel -I still am!

I remember when I was nine in 1933 that Adolf Hitler came to Munich to make a speech and there was a lot of trouble in the crowd and the police had to break it up. I wasn't there but I heard about it and saw things in the papers. There were no swastikas or marching soldiers at that time; that came later of course. Hitler was on the political campaign trail, he wanted our votes for his National Socialist Party. As well as his supporters there were also many in Bavaria who were anti-Nazi and did not want Hitler to come to power. In fact many of the local people demonstrated in the streets and wouldn't let him go into the main hall to make his speech. So he had to try to make his speech outside in the street. Many people were chanting 'Hau ab' (clear off!). People talked about Hitler a lot and many people were really against him. In fact he got arrested and put in prison although they soon let him out again. I remember hearing people who had seen him that day in Munich say that he was an ugly little dark haired man not at all like other tall, muscular and handsome Bavarian men to look at. Some say he ran away into the crowd when the trouble started. I even heard that he took off in an ambulance when the medics' backs were turned while they were helping injured people in the crowd. All that happened well before Hitler came to power in Germany of course. They say he chose Munich for his rally because he had some support in Bavaria during his rise to power, but certainly not from everyone at first, although Bavarians did eventually show support for him. I remember that in Bad Tölz there was an officers' training school for what was to become the Waffen-SS, the equivalent of Britain's Sandhurst or the USA's West Point. The school was actually opened in 1937 and operated until the end of World War II in 1945.

In the general election that followed Hitler only received a minority of the popular vote. But of course events soon changed after that. Hitler promised to save the German nation from economic gloom and turn the country into the Third Reich to last a thousand years. People fell for it and he was elected and declared himself Fuhrer (leader) of the German people. Once in power as Germany's Chancellor, Hitler changed the constitution and made himself a dictator with no need for further mandate from the people through elections. He also developed his power base in Bavaria and built a secure mountain stronghold retreat at Berchtesgarten known as the Eagle's Nest. Sepp and some of my friends told me about some of this but politics didn't interest me - still doesn't - I had other problems to contend with and I think that was true of many German people.

Living at home with my father was almost unbearable for me. By the time I was nine or ten I had run away from home at least four times. I didn't go too far; usually as far as Tegernsee, a holiday resort by a scenic lake about 20km away. I just wandered off and very often slept in a public toilet. I once got a job, by lying about my age, doing washing up in a hotel. I don't know how worried my parents were but I guess my father only missed me because he had to find a new 'slave' to feed the animals in the barn. To earn some extra cash I used to collect wild flowers called 'enzien' and sold bunches to tourists. Eventually someone in the hotel became suspicious and contacted the police. After all I was quite young. A policeman was sent out to question me and I told him why I had left home. He was quite sympathetic so I thought, maybe he can sort out my problems and things will get better for me. I was taken back home and I remember how the policeman gave my father a really good telling off for the way he had treated me. But then the policeman left of course and I was there and had to face my father. As you can imagine this incident didn't exactly make things any easier between me and my father. He was livid and took it out on me with a real fury. Things certainly didn't improve. I had to find a way to get out of there and get away from him.

The Enzien, or Gentian flower which Walter collected and sold to tourists when he ran away from home

Tegernsee - the holiday resort where
Walter ran to escape his father

Chapter 2
Runaway

I left school like most children at fourteen and went out to work in the nearby plywood factory. My mother died of a heart attack in the Spring of 1940 when I was fourteen. This was a really tragic time for our family and I was really emotionally affected by her death but also very worried about my situation. I had no mother to care for me and a father that hated me. Things were not looking good for me. To add to this the whole country was in a kind of madness because Hitler was now in power and everything seemed to be changing. Somehow we all got sucked into Hitler's Third Reich revolution through the National Socialist (Nazi) propaganda campaign. Boys of about my age were supposed to join the Hitler Jugend (Hitler Youth) movement and train ready to join the military when we became old enough. But I managed to get out of that somehow. I was never forced to join the Hitler Youth and that suited me just fine because I didn't have, and still don't have, any interest in politics. Eventually the German nation got to the point where we could do nothing to stop Hitler leading us into that terrible war with our neighbouring nations which had such profound repercussions for the whole world.

My life was in turmoil. The world seemed to have gone mad and I was completely unsettled and certainly fearful for my future at home with my father. I didn't discuss this with anyone but there seemed to be no good reason for me to stay living at home a moment longer. So I decided in the Autumn, just before my sixteenth birthday, to run away. Not like before but this time to do it properly and finally. I didn't feel nervous or undecided, I was certain and determined. My step brother, Sepp Gotz, had left home years before and at that time lived near Braunschweig (Brunswick) in a town called Wolfenbuttel in the north of Germany. He had always been good to me so I decided to put myself in his hands and start a new life up there. I had never been that far from home in my life, in fact the furthest from home that I'd ever been was to Munich when I had the hospital treatment as a small child. Now I was planning to go as far as north Germany - a completely different world as far as I, and most Bavarians that I knew, were concerned. There is quite a big cultural difference between north Germans and those from Bavaria in the south even to this day. The north was dominated by Prussian culture: militarism, the strong work ethic and the Protestant forms of Christianity. In the south most people's work is connected with the land. The northern Germans would say that we Bavarians are rustics and very conservative. We're certainly gentler folk, take life at a slower pace and most live and work close to the land and it's true that the majority of Bavarian people are Catholic.

It was September 1940. I woke up before everyone else in the house and crept downstairs and left without telling anyone. I took my bicycle; had a good one by then because I had saved up and bought it myself. I didn't make any elaborate preparation, all I had with me were the clothes I stood up in: lederhosen, shirt, jacket and shoes. I had no bag of possessions, no food and no money with me. I didn't even have a map but I had a bit of knowledge of Germany from school geography lessons. What I did have was my common sense, a need to get away from my father and a strong will to survive. I left without a backward glance at the house and not a single regret. I set off north cycling towards Wolfenbuttel which was about 600km north of Bad Tölz. When I think about it now it was quite a crazy thing to do to make a journey of that distance on a bike travelling through, what to me were alien lands, with no provisions or equipment of any kind, not to mention the fact that I had been a cripple only a few years earlier. The truth is, crazy or not, I did do it. Perhaps the years of collecting grass on my bike had strengthened me for this epic ride.

I knew that petrol filling stations in Germany at that time, in the early days of motoring, had maps of the German road network displayed on their walls to help motorists find their way. So I could go from one town or village to the next without getting lost by just looking at the road map, remembering the next place to aim for and then looking out for road signs. The journey took me only four days so I must have covered about 150km (about 100 miles) each day. No time for sight seeing or enjoying the views. Instead I had my head down and rode as fast as I could until I reached the next town or village. I stopped each night when it became dark and sought out a quiet barn with hay in and settled down for the night. No one ever found me. Remember, I didn't take any food with me and had no money to buy food but, as it was Autumn, there was plenty of fruit on the trees by the roadside so I ate mainly apples which I picked on the way. This was second nature to me as I'd been collecting by roadsides to feed the animals in the barn since I was seven years old.

As soon as it became light each day I got back on my bicycle and continued heading north. I can't remember much about the journey but I do remember seeing war planes flying overhead. One of these was a British Wellington bomber. You could always tell the British bombers from our own. The engine sound was quite different. This one was actually on fire, it must have been hit by one of our fighters or anti-aircraft guns. I saw it crash-land in a field. There was nothing I could do and I didn't want to be involved with any officials who might send me back home. So I continued on my way.

On the fourth night, I must have been getting quite near my destination by then, I met a strange old woman at the side of the road who stopped me. I remember her quite clearly. She looked exactly like how I had imagined a witch would look when I was a small child. She was bent over and walking with a crooked old stick. Her face was wrinkled and warty and her nose was hooked. She called out to me in a cackling voice so I went over to her. She seemed friendly enough and actually offered me her spare bedroom for the night. She also gave me something to drink and a sandwich. I couldn't pay her because I had no money but she didn't seem to care about that. As it was getting late and I would have to stop for the night soon anyway I took her up on the offer of a bed. Her house was like something out of the ark and a complete wreck inside and the place stank of something horrid. She lit a candle and ushered me upstairs where there was a spare bedroom and left me alone. I quickly prepared for bed and climbed in between the grubby damp sheets and blew out the candle. Everything was fine for a while and then, just as I was about to nod off, I started to hear noises. At first I couldn't make out what the sounds were and I lay awake wondering what they could be. Is she really a witch and is she casting spells to do something nasty to me? Perhaps

42

the house is haunted with ghosts and poltergeists. Then I felt something moving on the blanket and then on my face. What could this be? I was getting really scared with all theses thoughts and my hands were shaking but somehow I managed to light the candle. Mice! They were everywhere, running around the floor and over my bed. At least it wasn't anything spooky but still I couldn't get to sleep at all that night with the room so full of mice scampering all over the place, including over me, all night long. I got out of bed at first light having not slept a wink all night and certainly not refreshed much at all. I decided to slip out before the old woman got up in case there were other horrors awaiting me in that weird house. I didn't fancy eating any more of her food - goodness knows how many mice might have peed on it! I found my bike outside and set off as fast as I could to continue my journey. Later that day I reached the outskirts of Wolfenbuttel. I had made it to my destination.

Wolfenbuttel is a not a big town but it's easy to get lost in any town if you're not familiar with it. However, I had a note of Sepp's address which I can still remember to this day: Gotteslager 5, Wolfenbuttel. I have a tongue in my head so I managed to get directions. Mind you the people spoke with a very different accent from mine and I felt a bit like a foreign visitor. My step brother Sepp's house was a bungalow just outside the town boundary. He had moved to live there a few years before. His surname was Gotz and he was a bit older than me. At that time he was about twenty four and was married already and working as a painter and decorator in the town. I had always got on well with Sepp and had never forgotten how it was he who had always taken me to hospital in Munich when I had the surgery and treatment for my legs as a small child. When I arrived Sepp was out but his wife, who I had never met before, welcomed me in. It was a strange feeling to be in a house and feel at ease. Sepp and his wife were kind to me and let me live with them for as long as I wanted. As it turned out I lived with them for about two years. It was the first time I had actually experienced the feeling people get when they say 'I feel at home here'. I had definitely done the right thing coming here. My little adventure was well worth it.

I got a job at the local Fokker aeroplane factory at Bussing. The factory was manufacturing Fokker Wolf fighter planes at the time and I was put to work on the engine manufacturing line. This was completely different work from what I was used to but I soon adapted to it. I had to travel from Wolfenbuttel to the factory on a bus every day. The pay compared well with what I was used to so the money I earned easily covered my rent for Sepp. It felt good to be my own man, earning a living and paying my way. I was so content and so relieved to be well away from the troubles I had suffered in Bad Tölz that for the first six months that I was in Wolfenbuttel I made no attempt to contact my father. And as far as I know he made no attempt to find me. After six months I wrote to him requesting him to send me the small amount of money I had saved in a bank in Bad Tölz. He never replied and I never received that money. I did hear later on from Eddi that not long after my departure my father had sold all the animals in the barn and that there had been a succession of women who had moved in with him.

Those years with Sepp and his wife I remember as being very good times. I got on with my brother and his wife 'like a house on fire' and have happy memories of that time. There was a war going on but it didn't really affect me much. I had a home and a job and money in my pockets and best of all no father around to make my life a misery. I enjoyed my work at the Fokker factory and it seemed natural to me that I should learn to fly planes since I knew quite a bit about how they were built. So I took the opportunity offered to me to join the German equivalent of the Air Cadets and had free flying lessons near the factory every Sunday. I really enjoyed this and really wanted to be a flyer. At first I was taught how to fly a glider and pretty soon I progressed to flying bi-planes. They were considered to be old technology and very slow by then of course but it was all good experience for me. By the time I was seventeen and a half I had earned my pilots' licence. It never occurred to me that I was part of the huge armaments build-up ordered by Hitler. For me learning to fly was a great new opportunity for a daredevil like me to have more adventures. I was feeling very good about myself for the first time in my life. Everything seemed to be going really well and that feeling was something quite new to me. I'm not sure that I had realised it at the time but by becoming a pilot I had become a very valuable asset for Hitler's war strategy.

I wasn't interested in politics and not really bothered about what was going on in the world beyond. Just like the majority of ordinary German people I just got on with my life and my job and left politics to the politicians. We had been through some tough times as a nation. Unemployment had been pretty bad, there had been shortages of just about everything in the shops. Life was tough for most people. That's how Hitler got elected I suppose; he promised something better for the ordinary German people and we fell for it as a nation. And it's true to say that living standards did improve under Hitler. There were no more shortages of food and other essentials in the shops and we had once again become a proud nation, as good as, or if Hitler's propaganda was to be believed (and it was by more and more of us), better than the rest of the world. Many were now thinking that this Fuhrer may have some pretty nasty ways of doing things but at least he's brought us out of the depression and is giving us new hope for the future. Perhaps we are the master race after all, just like he tells us. Whatever else we were much better off than we were before he became German Chancellor.

Chapter 3
War Service with the Luftwaffe at Stalingrad

Soon after gaining my pilot's licence I was 'called up'. So I had to give in my notice at the Fokker factory. I wasn't concerned about going into the Luftwaffe, after all young men all over the country were being conscripted into the armed forces. Not only that but I had a naturally adventurous nature and was pretty fearless so this seemed to me like an invitation to a great adventure. Add to this the fact that the war had been going Germany's way for most of the time up to then so what was there to worry about? Before joining my unit I had about a week's leave to sort things out. I decided to take the opportunity to visit my brother Eddi who, by then, was working as a butcher in Rudesheim in the

Rhineland. I had always got on well with him and, as I hadn't seen him for quite a long time, decided to put that right before doing my duty to the Fatherland.

There's quite an interesting story as to how Eddi came to live in Rudesheim. A year or so before then the owners of a butcher's shop in Rudesheim had been on holiday in Bad Tölz and met

Eddi while they were there. They took a liking to him and he to them. At the time Eddi was only thirteen but it was agreed that he should go with them to live in Rudesheim, finish off his schooling there and at the same time begin to learn their family trade as a butcher. Sounds a bit strange I know but that's what happened. Remember my mother was dead and obviously my father had made no objection to the arrangement. He probably thought "one less mouth to feed".

For my visit to Eddi my plan was to cycle to Rudesheim, after all I was used to long cycle journeys by now! I stayed overnight in barns just like I did before but this time there was no old woman and no mice! It took me about three days. I must have been better prepared for the journey than before and certainly had some money in my pocket this time. It was 1940 so Eddi must have been fifteen years old. I had always got on well with him and had an enjoyable week in his company while I was there with him. It was my first time in the Rhineland and I remember seeing the River Rhine which was much wider than any river I'd ever seen before - full of heavy barges carrying goods like coal in either direction between Switzerland and Holland and places in between. It was good to have a little holiday. After all I'd never had one before, and it was good to spend time with Eddi. After a week there it was time for me to report to my Luftwaffe unit. I sold my bike to Eddi for a few Reichmark and took the train back to Braunschweig. Eddi stayed in Rudesheim until he was 'called up'. He joined the Wehrmacht (army) just before the end of the war. After the war he met his future wife, Marta who was a refugee from Czechoslovakia and they moved back to Munich where he set up business as a butcher once again. He is the only member of my family that I kept in touch with.

I was conscripted into the Luftwaffe as a pilot with the rank 'Gefleiter' with one stripe on my arm. I was posted to Bussing, an air base near Braunsweig, and received six month's intensive training flying Junkers 87 'Stuka' dive bombers. Stukas were not every pilot's favourite airplane by any means. They represented out of date technology and were not easy to handle. What's more pilots thought of them as death traps. What they were good at was dive bombing enemy targets for which they had gained a terrifying reputation. I didn't mind flying them at all. I wasn't the sort to be scared. I just got on with the job.

Even though I was stationed near Sepp's house I lived on the air base in barracks with about a dozen other airmen. There was a strict regime in there. We got up at 6am and spent an hour on 'spit and polish' jobs before breakfast. We had to put up with those 'stand to attention' inspections. By 8am we were flying and flew most of the day. Flying was good. I had no complaints about that but it was not long after this that petrol shortages meant that we couldn't fly so often. The war was not going quite so well for us so it appeared. Valuable fuel was needed at the Russian front line and that's where I soon found myself. During my training I became sick one day so was taken to the sick bay. There was a problem with my breathing. It was decided to send me to the main hospital in Berlin for medical tests. After tests the doctor gave me some tablets and sent me back to Bussing. I didn't stay there overnight so I was only in Berlin a few hours and that was the only time I have ever been to that city. I can't remember much about my time there as it was so short but I did see some American bombers flying over and I heard the bombs screaming down and exploding nearby. The hospital was not hit that time though. Berlin is a very different city from Munich; the people are completely different - we are like two different races of people and even though Berlin was our country's capital city it somehow felt foreign to me. I never had any desire to go to Berlin again and never have done so.

In 1942, when I was eighteen, I was posted to the Russian front near Stalingrad. By this stage of the war Hitler had already double-crossed Stalin and the Russians, Germany's former ally, and we were now fighting the Russians on the Eastern Front. I flew my Stuka over in short 'hops' to the base with the squadron. We had a leading aircraft with a pilot who knew his way there and had a map to follow. We just followed that aircraft. That's how it was done in those days. Pilots have it easy nowadays. Stukas were designed for short distance attack so had relatively small fuel tanks. Consequently we had to stop a few times on the way to re-fuel. I remember that one of the refuelling stops was at Krakow in Poland which we had occupied early on in the war. We'd made quite a mess of the city from what I saw looking down. After a few more hops we landed near Stalingrad. Stukas were used in many battle dive bombing scenarios but at Stalingrad we were dive bombing Russian tanks.

The Battle of Stalingrad - historical footnote:
The city of Stalingrad was originally called Tsaritsyn, but adopted Stalin's name during his dictatorship from 1924-53. (After the was it became Volgograd under Krushchev's process of deStalinisation.) The Battle of Stalingrad was probably the turning point in World War II in Europe. The battle at Stalingrad bled the German army dry in Russia and after this defeat, the German Army was in full retreat. One of the ironies of the war is that the German Sixth Army need not have

become entangled in Stanlingrad. Army Groups A and B were well on their way to the Caucasus in southwest Russia when Hitler ordered an attack on Stalingrad. Some historians believe that Hitler ordered the taking of Stalingrad simply because of the name of the city and Hitler's hatred of Joseph Stalin. For the same reason Stalin ordered that the city had to be saved.

The Battle for Stalingrad was fought during the winter of 1942 to 1943. In September 1942, the German commander of the Sixth Army, General Paulus, assisted by the Fourth Panzer Army, advanced on the city of Stalingrad. His primary task was to secure the oil fields in the Caucasus and to do this, Paulus was ordered by Hitler to take Stalingrad. The Germans final target was to have been Baku. Stalingrad was also an important target as it was Russia's centre of communications in the south as well as being a centre for manufacturing.

In early September 1942, the German Army advanced to the city. The Russians, already devastated by the power of Blitzkrieg during Operation Barbarossa, had to make a stand especially as the city was named after the Russian leader, Joseph Stalin. For simple reasons of morale, the Russians could not let this city fall. Likewise, the Russians could not let the Germans get hold of the oil fields in the Caucasus. Stalin's order was "Not a step backwards". The battle for the city descended into one of the most brutal in World War II. Individual streets were fought over using hand-to-hand combat. The Germans took a great deal of the city but they failed to fully assert their authority. Areas captured by the Germans during the day, were re-taken by the Russians at night. On November 19th, the Russians were in a position whereby they could launch a

counter-offensive. Marshal Zhukov used six armies of one million men to surround the city. The German army was thus trapped in Stalingrad. The German commander, General von Paulus, could have broken out of this trap in the first stages of Zhukov's attack but was forbidden from doing so by Hitler. Supreme Commander (Hitler) to 6 Army, January 24, 1943 "Surrender is forbidden. 6 Army will hold their positions to the last man and the last round and by their heroic endurance will make an unforgettable contribution towards the establishment of a defensive front and the salvation of the Western world." *Hitler's communication with von Paulus.*

Unable to break out, the Germans also had to face the winter. Temperatures dropped to well below zero and food, ammunition and heat were in short supply.

"My hands are done for, and have been ever so since the beginning of December. The little finger of my left hand is

missing and, what's even worse, the three middle fingers of my right one are frozen. I can only hold my mug with my thumb and little finger. I'm pretty helpless; only when a man has lost any fingers does he see how much he needs them for the smallest jobs. The best thing I can do with the little finger is to shoot with it. My hands are finished." **Anonymous German soldier**

Generalfeldmarschall Friedrich Paulus (left),
with his chief of staff, Generalleutnant Arthur Schmidt
(centre) and his aide, Wilhelm Adam (right),
after their surrender.

Hitler ordered that Paulus should command his men to fight to the last bullet, and to encourage Paulus, he promoted him to Field Marshal. However, by the end of January 1943, the Germans could do nothing else but surrender. Paulus surrendered the army in the southern sector on January 31st while General Schreck surrendered the northern group on February 2nd, 1943. The failure of the German Army was nothing short of a disaster. A complete army group was lost at Stalingrad and 91,000 Germans were taken prisoner. With such a massive loss of manpower and equipment, the Germans simply did not have enough resources to cope with the Russian advance to Germany when it came. Despite resistance in parts - such as at Kursk - they were in retreat on the Eastern Front from February 1943 on. In his fury, Hitler ordered a day's national mourning in Germany, not for the men lost at the battle, but for the shame von Paulus had brought on the Wehrmacht and Germany. Paulus was also stripped of his rank to emphasise Hitler's anger with him

Back to my story ....

I arrived at the airbase in October when winter was approaching. It wasn't a proper air field and we only had a road that we had captured as a runway as well as buildings nearby which we used as barracks. We had about forty Stukas and there must have been about two hundred men - flyers and ground crew. We were about ten minutes flying time from the front line at Stalingrad. Our job was to dive-bomb Russian tanks. Flying low over the area I was able to see the battle going on below me. It was really cold when winter arrived. We lived in really harsh conditions with hardly any heat and no comforts at all. Every morning when we were woken up by the sergeant we were made to strip 'bollock naked' and go outside in the freezing cold for morning exercises, including running barefoot in the deep snow and ice. I was told it was 40 degrees below freezing some days. These exercises were intended to toughen us up for fighting in these incredibly harsh conditions and to be ready to face the ferocious Russian enemy. I remember that some of my fellow airmen refused to follow the deep freeze physical exercise orders. Ironically it was actually some of these men who perished in the depth of a Russian winter whilst we blokes who had been toughened up somehow survived .

My job while I was there was to Fly Junkers 87 'Stuka' dive bomber missions. A Stuka had two seats, one behind the other. As pilot I sat in front and Hans, my machine gunner, behind me. The cockpit was small and as I'm a big bloke it was a very tight fit for me. Hans and I usually flew the same plane unless of course I had crash-landed it. But that plane and I had flown so many missions and been hit by anti-aircraft fire so many times that it was a real mess with shrapnel and holes all over the fuselage and wings and the Perspex canopy peppered with bullet holes; It was like flying in a colander! I had a joystick shaped a bit like bicycle handlebars and two pedals, one for pulling out of a dive and the other was like an accelerator on a car. There were instruments on board of course, like an altimeter and compass, and there was also a radio for communication between the pilot and ground crew. There was also a machine gun for the pilot to use. It fired forwards from the centre of the propeller. These aircraft carried five bombs: a large one under the fuselage and two smaller bombs under each wing. We were trained to fly directly towards our target and at the last minute to release a bomb and then turn away sharply. The bomb's momentum allowed it to continue to the target - that's if we got everything right.

Stukas were designed for short flying missions. They had a range of only about 150 miles because they didn't carry much fuel unlike say a Fokker Wolf which carried enough fuel to escort Dornier bombers to English cities and back. I did fly a Fokker Wolf occasionally. Now that was a really fast plane - faster than a Spitfire although I'm told that a Spitfire was more manoeuvrable than a Fokker until the wing was redesigned, copying the Spitfire design. There is a story that Douglas Bader, the well-known British flying ace, flew his Spitfire to join a formation group of Fokkers mistaking them for Spitfires until he noticed the German crosses on the other aircraft! That must have given him a bit of a shock! So Stuka dive bomber aircraft were only able to fly for about 30 minutes at a time and their normal flying speed was only about 300mph due to the old design and suffering the constant drag of having fixed landing wheels. So we also were always based near our targets and at Stalingrad our targets were Russian tanks.

We flew in a group of about a dozen planes with the leader (Kapitan) giving orders over the radio. What I had to do was locate the target, point the aircraft's nose at it, and then dive down really fast - with the help of gravity I could reach well over 5OOmph. When a Stuka was in a dive it made a hell of a loud screaming noise. In fact, the plane was designed to make this noise with sirens built into the wings - it must have scared the pants off the poor blighters below. When I had the plane lined up with the target I'd release one of the five bombs and that also activated an automatic pre-set steep banking manoeuvre of the plane away from the target. I would repeat this manoeuvre until all five bombs were deployed. After that I would keep the aircraft fairly low to avoid anti-aircraft fire and make my way back to base, usually about 10 minutes flying time away. Because Stukas were only used in these kinds of operations I only ever saw other Luftwaffe planes and never an enemy aircraft at any time that I was up.

Some background information about Junker Stuka Dive Bombers and their pilots:

The missions of the dive bomber pilots were simpler than those of the conventional bomber and could be monotonous as one mission was very much the same as another. It is said that Stuka pilots were less ready than other Luftwaffe pilots to talk about their operational experiences. The Ju-87 Stuka was not very manoeuvrable and only by turning as tightly as possible could it avoid the much faster enemy aircraft. A great deal was expected of Stuka pilots and there was little in the way of recognition for them in return. Never-the-less these airman rarely sought transfers to other branches of the Luftwaffe and developed a strong loyalty and love of their aircraft and the job they were doing even many found this attitude incomprehensible. The classic picture of a Stuka pilot was cool, well balanced, phlegmatic, having a strong sense of duty and an aggressive spirit. One of the best known Stuka leader pilots was Oberstleutnant Kuhlmey known as the 'Prince of Bir Hacheim'. He had a friendly nature with cautious reserve and a strong sense of self-worth, inner stability together with mental prowess and acuity. All Stuka pilots flew like the devil, stayed in tight formation and together they fought off enemy fighter attacks. Amongst the most prominent Stuka pilots were Oskar

Dinort, Hubertus Hitschold, Walter Sigel and Karl Henze. The most highly decorated member of the German armed forces in WWII was actually a Stuka pilot: Hans-Ulrich Rudel.

Back to my story............
On one of my sorties my plane was hit by Russian anti-aircraft fire. I started to go down but I managed to bring the aircraft around and very fortunately for me managed to crash-land and even more fortunately for me, the crash landing was behind the German lines. We had been warned in our training that for German airmen to be captured by Russians meant certain death so I didn't bail out using the ejector seat and parachute, in fact I never used these in any of my missions, instead I used all my skills as a pilot to avoid landing behind the Russian lines. You can't really be trained on how to crash land you just have to make it up as you go along and follow your instincts depending on the state of the aircraft and the ground and weather conditions. The important thing is to keep the aircraft level and find a landing spot with no obstacles such as trees or buildings.

My plane ended up with its nose buried in the ground and was wrecked but it didn't catch fire fortunately probably because Stukas didn't carry much fuel on board. Both my buddy and I got out alive and managed to escape with only comparatively minor injuries. I had been shot in my arm and leg and ended up in a field hospital about 50km behind the front line. I was in there for about three weeks and made a couple of friends in there. I can't remember their names now though.

I suffered no permanent injuries and made a good recovery. After being discharged from hospital I was sent

STUKAS IM FLUG

back to the air base and resumed dive bombing missions.

In November 1942 the Red Army launched Operation Uranus which resulted in the Germans in the city of Stalingrad being entirely surrounded. Hitler ordered that the army stay put in Stalingrad and make no attempt to break out; instead, attempts were made to supply the army by air and to break the encirclement from the outside.

I was flying transport aircraft to get the supplies in and the injured soldiers out. As the ground was covered in snow and ice, the planes were fitted with snow skids. As I was picking up speed for take-off I found that I could not get off the ground and when I looked out of the windows I saw that the wings were covered with troops desperate to get out. As I gained more speed one-by-one they fell off the wings.

Above and below:
The Abbey of Monte Cassino after its decimation in 1944

Chapter 4
Monte Cassino

After a few weeks I was posted to Monte Cassino in Italy, where there was fierce fighting against the Allies.

The Battle of Monte Cassino - historical footnote:
The Battle of Monte Cassino (also known as the Battle for Rome and the Battle for Cassino) was a costly series of four battles during World War II, fought by the Allies with the intention of breaking through the Winter Line and seizing Rome. American and British troops had landed in the south of Italy and had advanced north. By the beginning of 1944, the western half of the line was being anchored by Germans holding the Rapido, Liri and Garigliano valleys and certain surrounding peaks and ridges, together known as the Gustav Line. The Germans had not occupied the historic hilltop abbey of Monte Cassino, founded in AD 524 by Benedict of Nursia. This magnificent abbey dominated the town of Cassino and the entrances to the Liri and Rapido valleys. The German military had, however, created defensive positions set into the steep slopes below the abbey walls. On 15 February the monastery, high on a peak overlooking the town of Cassino, was destroyed by 1,400 tons of bombs dropped by American bombers. The bombing was based on the fear that the abbey was being used as a lookout post for the German defenders. Two days after the bombing, German paratroopers took up positions in the ruins; the destruction caused by the bombing and the resulting jagged wasteland of rubble gave troops

improved protection from air and artillery attack making it a more viable defensive position. From 17 January to 18 May, the Gustav defences were assaulted four times by Allied troops. For the last of these the Allies gathered 20 divisions for a major assault along a twenty mile front and drove the German defenders from their positions; but at a high cost.

Back to my story again ....

   When I landed my aircraft at Monte Cassino there was a standoff and a huge battle was going on. The airstrip at the base was just a grass runway. Our job was to bomb a harbour and allied shipping on the east coast. I think it was at Brindisi. Not long after arriving there and carrying out bombing sorties I got shot down again and another of my planes was wrecked. Once again I managed to crash-land behind German lines. This time my injuries meant I had to be sent back to the nearest main hospital in Germany at Munich for treatment. During my recovery I quickly regained strength and, as this Munich hospital was quite near my home town, I requested that I be moved to the hospital at Bad Tölz and my request was granted. I remember that my brothers Otto and Eddi and some of my old friends came to visit me in hospital - but not my father. I hadn't been in contact with him for years. Actually I lost contact with many people I had known. There was a war on, towns were being bombed day and night - it was chaos in Germany. People lost touch; they didn't know where friends and family might be or whether they were still alive. Everything was in turmoil and everyone was just too busy just trying to stay alive. That's what war does to you

The present cathedral of Montecassino was built and rebuilt several times, and rather expanded over the centuries. The present cathedral was born after the most recent destruction took place during the Battle of Monte Cassino in 1944, and was reconstructed according to the design of the 17th / 18th century cathedral, with some original elements surviving the bombing.

Chapter 5
Stalingrad again

I was sent back to Italy after a few weeks in hospital. But not very long after that I was shot down again and ended up in a hospital in Italy. Mussolini was the Italian dictator and Italy was fighting alongside Hitler's Germany at that time. After being stationed for six more months in Italy, much of that time in hospital or grounded during my recovery, I was posted to Holland near Eindhoven for more training. I think this was about the same time that Italy surrendered to the Allied Forces. I also had to undergo some medical tests including tests on my eyesight. For some reason which I didn't understand my friend Franz Muller, who was also a Stuka pilot, and I were both sent to Paris for these tests. Of course France had been occupied by German forces by then so it was like being sent to a German city I suppose but I can't remember much about it. I stayed at the Paris hospital for one night and was declared fit to carry on flying. I was then sent back to my Stuka unit in Holland. Not long after that my posting was changed and I was off to Poland with the Stuka unit. The planes were partly dismantled and loaded on to a train and we headed east. I remember one of the stops that we made on the journey was at Breslau. At that time Breslau was a German city in the district called Silesien (Silesia) near the border with Poland. After the war that area, which was industrially very important, became part of Poland and Breslau was re-named Wroclaw. It was a large, typically German city when I went there but after the war when Silesia was ceded to Poland the city was subjected to ruthless de-Germanification with mass deportations of German inhabitants. I'm told that if you visit Wroclaw nowadays you would be hard pressed to find any reminders of its German origins. Eventually we arrived back at the same airfield where I'd been posted last time, near Stalingrad.

I wasn't best pleased to be back in the freezing Russian weather again and the battle for Stalingrad was not going at all well for us Germans. I was flying Stuka bombing raids again but the Russians were a much more organised fighting force by that time and it wasn't long after I had started flying missions there that I was shot down for the fourth and last time. Once again I crash-landed and tragically my fellow airman was killed. This time I had been unable to control the landing as the aircraft would not respond to the controls. There was nothing I could do for the other guy. I was badly injured and, as always in these situations, there is a big risk that the aircraft will catch fire or explode so I needed to get away. When I got out of the wreckage I worked out my location from the maps with me. I found myself to be about 6 km behind Russian lines. I'm not easily frightened by anything but this was a very dangerous situation for me. If I was found by the Russians I would be shot for sure. There were plenty of stories of this happening to other Luftwaffe pilots. We had been given some basic training about surviving this sort of situation. I decided to hide during the day and move at night. That way there would be a chance that the Russians might not spot me. But I had to get as far away from the plane as possible because the Russians would certainly find that easily enough and probably start searching for me. It was incredibly cold, 40 degrees below zero. I was badly injured with bullet wounds in my shoulder and the side of my body and I was losing a lot of blood. I had no supplies of food or water. When I think back on that time it makes me shudder. It would have been easy to just give up but that's not my way. I was going to give this my best shot and made myself crawl somehow. Moving was extremely painful for me and I could only move a very short distance at a time but somehow I managed to crawl, painfully slowly, on my elbows and knees. After a night of this I was totally done in and it was as much as I could do to crawl into a hole in the snow and keep still and hopefully sleep for a while until it was dark again. I don't know how but I managed to keep this up for four long nights. By that time I had lost so much blood that I was as weak as a kitten and frozen to the marrow. The only drink available was the snow and there was plenty of that around fortunately. The pain from my injuries was excruciating but I have great determination and a strong sense of self-preservation so I kept going.

At the end of the fourth night of crawling I eventually reached the German lines. Imagine my relief to see German uniforms and friendly faces. My comrades were very surprised to see me alive, they had long ago given me up for dead. I was just as amazed to be alive as they were. In fact I was extremely fortunate to have survived that episode. As I was so weak and my injuries were fairly severe, after some treatment in the field hospital I was taken back to Germany and ended up in the hospital in Bad Tölz again.

Fortunately my injuries were not beyond the surgeons' skills and my own body's powers to heal so after a stay in hospital I was transferred to a military convalescent home. Every day I grew stronger so while I was convalescing I got permission to visit my old home in Bad Tölz. Unbeknown to me my father had remarried and when I knocked his new wife answered the door. I explained who I was and that I'd come to see Otto my brother. She wouldn't let me in and was really aggressive with me. I tried to reason with her but it was no good - she just slammed the door in my face. I got really mad then and pushed the door right off its hinges. The door fell right on top of her flattening her underneath it. Then I saw Otto who was sitting in the corner of the kitchen with a terrified expression on his face. He made no attempt to do anything. I felt all the anger, which had been bottled up in me for so many years, suddenly come rushing out. I was roaring at the top of my voice and started to smash up the furniture. I hated my father, I hated his new wife, I hated everything to do with him including the furniture that he had made. In a wild rage I started smashing up the place and demolished two wooden cabinets and a table and smashed the chairs across the room. There was such a commotion that the neighbours must have been alarmed and probably called my father because it was at this moment that he came storming into the house. He rushed at me with the look of a blood-thirsty maniac in his eyes. He had a knife in his hands and was swearing 'blue murder' - I'm sure he wanted to kill me. It was like one of those horror movies except this was really happening to me. We started to fight like wild animals. I had a bayonet with me and I defended myself against him with his knife. I caught him with the bayonet across the knuckles of his hand which was holding the knife, nearly severing his fingers. He gave out an enormous scream of pain. There was such a commotion going on that the neighbours had called the police. When the policeman arrived he managed to separate us and made us calm down but he took no further action. He

Walter's model Junkers JU 87 Stuka

announced that in his view the 'argument' was just a family matter and that he did not want to get involved. I suppose with the way the war was going this domestic incident was considered too trivial to waste valuable police time on. So, with everyone standing around 'gob-smacked' and my father nursing his bleeding hand, I just walked out and left them all to it and made my way back the convalescent home; some convalescence! In total, I was in Bad Tölz for about seven weeks. There was no further word from my family or the police and I never saw my father again after that day.

By then it was 1944 and there were seven of us airmen in the convalescent home attached to the hospital. The war was not going well for Germany and petrol was in very short supply. There was not enough fuel for the few remaining air-worthy aircraft left after the allied attack on our tanker fleet. Because of this all of us ended up being transferred to the Wehrmacht (Germany's army) and we were posted to Braunsweig. My flying days were at an end.

Chapter 6
War Service in the Wehrmacht

So now I was in the Wehrmacht, and a soldier. My army unit consisted of 120 men. We received just two week's army basic training and each of us was given a bicycle, as there was no fuel for army vehicles. We didn't even have enough proper weapons or ammunition; it was all rather sad and pathetic and not at all like we had imagined the army to be like. We were posted to Poland and then found out that orders had been confused and so soon after, in October 1944, we were taken by train to Holland near Eindhoven. Holland had been occupied by German forces for some years but the allies were fighting their way across from the west following the D-Day landings. On the journey to Eindhoven our train was attacked by British aircraft and we lost two men shot dead. I remember us shooting our rifles out of the train windows hoping to shoot down the Spitfires-some hope! The train managed to keep going and we eventually arrived in Eindhoven and found ourselves in barracks that was once a disused tobacco factory building. Soon after our arrival my unit was sent to the front line near Arnhem. For some reason, probably because I had such a collection of war wounds, the captain ordered me to stay behind to guard the unit's 120 bicycles. He said he would come back for me. I had no choice, orders are orders. I didn't know at the time but my unit got tied up in a dreadful battle.

Battle of Overloon- historical footnote:

The Battle of Overloon was a Second World War battle between Allied forces and the German army which took place in and around the village of Overloon in the south-east of the Netherlands between September 30 and October 18, 1944. The battle, which resulted in an Allied victory, ensued after the Allies launched Operation Aintree. The Allies went on to liberate the town of Venray. In September 1944, the Allies had launched Operation Market Garden, a major offensive from the Dutch-Belgian border across the south of the Netherlands through Eindhoven and Nijmegen towards the Rhine bridge at Arnhem, with the goal of crossing the Rhine and bypassing the Siegfried Line in preparation for the final drive towards Berlin. Allied airborne forces were defeated at the Rhine bridge in Arnhem and the advance stopped south of the Lower Rhine, resulting in a narrow salien that ran from the north of Belgium across the south-east of the Netherlands.

German forces attacked this salient from a bridgehead west of the bend in the river Meuse (known as Maas in Dutch) near the city of Venlo. The bridgehead was established by retreating German forces that were reinforced with troops arriving from nearby Germany by crossing the Meuse in Venlo. The western edge of this bridgehead ran through the Peel marshes, a fen area with marshy ground and several canals blocking an Allied advance. The Allies decided to attack the bridgehead from the north, and this meant they had to capture Overloon and Venray, which were on the road towards Venlo. Operation Aintree had the goal of securing the narrow salient the Allies had established between Eindhoven and Nijmegen during Operation Market Garden and destroying the German bridgehead west of the

Meuse, in preparation for the eventual Allied advance into the nearby German Rhineland. The battle of Overloon ensued as the Allies advanced from nearby positions southwards toward the village of Overloon. Following a failed attack on Overloon by the U.S. 7th Armoured Division, the British 3rd Infantry Division and the British 11th Armoured Division took over. Suffering heavy losses the Allies captured Overloon and moved towards Venray. The advance on Venray resulted in heavy losses, especially around the Loobeek creek, which was swollen due to heavy Autumn rains and was flooded and mined by the Germans. Casualties were heavy here among the First Battalion of the Royal Norfolk Regiment. During the battle, the village of Overloon was destroyed. In and around Overloon, some 2,500 soldiers died, making it one of the bloodiest battles in the Netherlands during the Second World War. It was also the only major tank battle ever fought on Dutch soil. Dozens of tanks, mainly British, were destroyed. Despite the fact that both Overloon and eventually Venray were taken by the Allies, the advance toward the bend of the Meuse near Venlo was postponed. This was due to the number of casualties the Allies had sustained and because troops were needed to secure more essential targets: the Scheldt estuary, leading to the vital port of Antwerp and the west of the province of North Brabant, in between Antwerp and the salient that had been established. The offensive was eventually resumed and by early December the German bridgehead west of the Meuse was destroyed.

Back to my story ....

While I was waiting there, guarding all those bikes, for what seemed ages a friendly Dutchman came up to me and offered to give me some food. He was quite chatty and spoke a little German and told me that he was interested in the bicycles, which were all fairly new and in quite good condition. He offered to pay me for them. At first I thought I'd get into real trouble with my captain if I did that but then he told me that the British had broken the German line and were on their way towards Eindhoven. He went on to tell me about the terrible battle which had wiped out the German soldiers and that the British were only about one mile away from where we were standing. From what he had just said to me it was clear that probably none of my unit was going to come back for me or their bikes. He asked me what I was going to do. What should I do? At first I decided to sell half the bicycles to him for a small sum thinking that maybe some of my unit would make it back and need the bikes. Then later, when I had thought things through, I decided that the only sensible course of action was to give myself up as a POW. After all it wouldn't look good to be charged with a black market offence either by my own officers or as a POW by the Allies. So I decided to give the money back to the Dutchman and told him to do what he wanted with all the bikes and to arrange for me to be taken prisoner by the British. He readily agreed and set off in the direction of the British camp. Not long after this he returned with two Scottish soldiers, dressed in full tartan regalia. I was arrested and taken to their camp. I don't know what happened to the bikes but I do know that from that moment my war was over; I was a POW. Later, in the compound, I met my unit captain and two other soldiers from the unit. They looked in a bad way and I found out from them that of the 120 men in my unit who left me looking after the bikes only those three had survived the battle. The unit had been virtually wiped out by Allied fire including flame throwers - I had been very lucky once again!

Chapter 7
Life as a POW

After my surrender to the British I was eventually taken across the English Channel to England. I remember it well as it was my birthday - 15 November 1944. We were herded into all sorts of craft and I remember that all my fellow prisoners were very quiet, almost peaceful. It was like we were all relieved that the war was over for us at last. We landed somewhere on the east coast and were herded into train carriages; not cattle trucks as I expected, there were proper seats. We were taken to a place near Wimbledon and herded into a barbed wire compound. I remember that it was raining most of the time and that I was there for two days with over 3,000 other German POWs. After that we were moved by train to a proper POW compound at an army camp near Blackpool. I reckon there were about 4,000 German POWs in that camp. The army barracks was surrounded by barbed wire and there were about a dozen guards on duty at any one time. The guards were generally quite friendly as long as we didn't give them any trouble. We didn't want trouble, we just wanted this nightmare war to end and to get back to our own lives again.

The regime wasn't too strict and after a while we relaxed enough to enjoy ourselves and even get up to some devilment from time to time. I remember that once, just for fun, we planned a surprise for our guards. At a given signal we grabbed the guards, took their guns and held them prisoner. We then marched them off to the camp commander. He knew what we were like and realised that this was harmless fun and not a rebellion. He treated the matter as a joke and just said "One German POW is more trouble than a dozen badly behaved British soldiers." I'm not sure that the guards enjoyed the joke as much but we got away with it anyway. I also remember one particular German POW who came in. He had only one leg. We greeted him and tried to show some sympathy for his injured state. He just said "Don't worry about me, I'll be out of here tomorrow". And he was. He escaped somehow but we heard later that eventually he was picked up in the Irish Republic; quite a good escape run for a man with only one leg.

I was in the camp near Blackpool for about 6 months when we were moved out in groups. About 500 of us were taken south. I ended up in a POW camp near Shaftesbury in Dorset. It was at Motcombe Park on West Field. Temporary buildings had been erected on the site of a school. At that time there were dozens of POW camps in Britain. We lived in the camp at night and during the day we were taken out to local farms for forced labour. I was sent on my own to East Orchard Farm where I had the job of feeding 500 pigs. In the mornings I used to go with the farmer in his lorry to the camp and other places to get swill to feed the pigs. Once, I remember the farmer took out his handkerchief from his pocket to blow his nose and a revolver fell out on to the floor. I spotted this of course. The farmer was very edgy and quite obviously embarrassed about this. I could speak a bit of English by that time so I said to him "You don't need that gun to protect yourself from me - if I had wanted to kill you I would have done it a long time ago." He got the message and laughed. We got on really well from that day on. I was there for about 6 months. I didn't feel like a prisoner really and became quite content living and working out in the countryside.

One damp foggy morning, while I was working at that farm, the farmer's wife from the neighbouring farm came running up to me in a real state. She was gasping and hardly able to speak but managed to get me to understand that she wanted me to come quickly because her son had had an accident. In fact he had fallen down the well at their farm. It never occurred to me in any way odd that she asked me, a German POW, rather than anyone else for help. Of course I went with her straight away. When I arrived there were about half a dozen men staring hopelessly down the well shaft but none of them would go down. They were saying that it was too dangerous; you could drown or die of suffocation, and the bloke had probably drowned down there already. I couldn't understand why nobody was trying to save him. It was 60 feet deep and there was an iron ladder fixed to the side. I didn't hang about. I pushed the other blokes aside and got right up to the top of the well. grabbed the rope they had and told them to hang on to the end. I then started going down the ladder. When I had gone down about 20 feet I noticed that it was hard to breathe; there was very little air down there. I kept going down and eventually reached the man at the bottom. It was pitch dark and wet and my lungs were gasping for air. I could see that the man's head wasn't completely underwater but he wasn't moving either. It was so dark I couldn't tell how bad he was but he was making some quiet groaning noises. Just by feeling my way I managed to tie the end of the rope around his body and shouted to the others to haul him up. I felt him pass me as he was pulled up and then I climbed back up the ladder. When I got to the top I was gasping for air after being down in that

Mr. Walter Schnitzer.

"Riversdale"
Stour Provost
Gillingham
Dorset

Please accept our Sincere
and Grateful Thanks for
your Kind and Brave deed
in the rescue of my Son. H. G. Hartnell.
on October 20th 1946.

From Mr & Mrs. S. Hartnell + Family.

Swanscombe
East Orchard.

To Walter.
Just a small present
for your kind & brave deed
that you did for me have not
had the chance of seeing you
before.

From Mrs H. Hartnell

Swanscombe
East Orchard.

To Walter.
Just a small present
for your kind & brave deed
that you did for me have not
had the chance of seeing you
before.

From Mrs H. Hartnell.

airless place. In the light of day I could see the strange colour of the man's face. Nowadays we'd know that what he needed was resuscitation but none of us knew much about things like that in those days. Someone had sent for a doctor but all we could do in the meantime was to make the man as comfortable as possible and watch over him as life gradually ebbed away from him. By the time the doctor arrived the farmer's son was pronounced dead. He had either suffocated because there was not enough air down at the bottom of the well or suffered some internal injury through the fall. I had to sit down to recover for about ten minutes after my time down there. Of course it was a great shame that the farmer's son's life was lost and I felt so sad for the family, especially the mother. I never once thought of him as one of the enemy, he was another human being and I felt the same sorrow as if he'd been a fellow German. I also thought how lucky I was to have survived after that experience down that well with hardly any air to breathe. In fact of all the close shaves I've had in my life, and there have been quite a few as you know, that was probably the nearest I came to death myself.

There was an inquest into the death sometime after and I was called to give evidence to the coroner. He asked me "How was it that you, as one of our country's enemies, were the one to go down to save this British man?" I replied: "Enemy? Who is the worst enemy you or me - would you have tried to save me?" The coroner said he'd consider sending me back to Germany for being so insolent but he didn't. I think he must have given some careful thought to what I had said. The farmer's wife was obviously grief-stricken but after a few days, when she had recovered somewhat, she gave me chocolates, cigarettes and a wallet with £20 and two hand-written notes thanking me.

One note was from the dead man's mother asking me to accept her grateful thanks for the kind and brave deed, as she put it, in the rescue of her son. She signed it Mr & Mrs S Hartnell and family. Their address was Riversdale, Stour Provost, Gillingham, Dorset. The other note was from Mrs H Hartness of Swainscombe, East Orchard, where I was working. She was the dead man's wife. In her note with her present she says that it was a kind and brave deed that I did for her. What a sad day that was for that family. I have kept the wallet and the notes to this day - they bring back very strong memories for me

German Prisoners of War pick swedes in a field near their PoW camp, somewhere in Britain. Two horses can also be seen in the field.
mage by Ministry of Information Photo Division Photographer [Public domain], via Wikimedia Commons

German Prisoners of War in Britain- Everyday Life at a German Pow Camp, UK, 1945
mage by Ministry of Information Photo Division Photographer [Public domain], via Wikimedia Commons

Chapter 8
After the war was over

After I had been at the farm for a few months the war came to an end and I was allowed to move from the POW camp to live at the farm. I guess many POWs were repatriated to Germany but I decided to stay, at least for the time being. The farmer provided me with what he called a caravan. It was actually a crudely converted cattle trailer into which he'd fitted a bunk bed and a few other essentials. There was a paraffin stove which I used for cooking and to heat the place. One night it was so cold that I left the paraffin stove burning when I went to bed. I woke up in the middle of the night coughing and spluttering. The 'caravan' was full of black smoke and I could hardly breathe. I blew out the flame and opened the door to get some air in. When I looked at myself in the mirror I was black all over. I could have suffocated in the night - yet another one of my lucky escapes.

On the farm there was a dairyman. His job was to milk the cows, fill the churns, and then thoroughly clean the milking parlour including the milking machines. He was a lazy bugger. He didn't bother with the cleaning up especially if there was a horse race on at Wincanton or Salisbury. He used to say to me "You do it!", and then just clear off to the racecourse. Well I did do it. I don't know why, but I did. On one occasion when he had gone off to the races and left me to do his work I was late arriving at the milking parlour and another farm hand shouted at me because I hadn't cleaned up. He balled out "You lazy bloody Nazi." The farmer heard this and came in. I felt anger swell up inside me. I wasn't going to be accused of not doing a job which wasn't even mine to do and I was not going to be racially abused by anyone. I said nothing, I just grabbed the farm hand who had called me a Nazi by his collar and the seat of his trousers and threw him through the trap door where the milk churns went. There was a hell of a din with him screaming and buckets and everything crashing. The farmer watched all this but said nothing, he just turned and walked. Maybe he thought I was going to do the same to him or more likely he thought the bloke got what he deserved. The farmer and I actually got on like a house on fire from that day onwards but that farm worker kept his distance from me. From that day on and he certainly never ever called me a Nazi again.

I wasn't the only ex POW who had decided to stay on in Britain after the war. There were quite a few about and I got to know a number of other German blokes who were working in neighbouring farms. It was 1946, so there were no guards watching over us as we weren't POWs any more. We were free to go back to Germany if we wanted to, but what was there back in Germany for us? We'd seen the newspapers and heard that the whole country was in a terrible mess, much worse than Britain in fact. People often talk about the terrible aftermath of the war in Britain but it was even worse over there. I've seen photos of German cities where there's hardly one building still standing after the Allied bombing raids. Germany was a defeated nation and the country was in chaos. People were like refugees trying to find a place to live among piles of rubble. There were terrible food shortages and there were no jobs. The country was broken and everyone was at rock-bottom. I was quite happy with my lot on the farm in a nice corner of England. Even though I was German, I encountered very little resentment or hostility from locals. Most people were pleasant and some were quite kind to me. I had a home of sorts, I had food to eat and 2 shillings a week pay (that's just 10p now, but money went a lot further in those days!). I decided to stay put in England.

I left the farm near Shaftesbury and moved near to Wincanton. I can't remember the circumstances for my move; anyway I was working at another farm. One day I noticed that a field on a neighbouring farm was full of rabbits. You know how rabbit population numbers seem to follow a cycle. Well this must have been a boom year for rabbits as there were hundreds of them that year. I found the farmer who owned that field and said "If you lend me a gun I'll shoot some rabbits so we can all have meat for dinner." Meat and lots of other things were rationed at that time of course and meat was always scarce. The farmer knew I had been a German POW of course and gave me an 'old fashioned' glance as much as to say 'Do you think I was born yesterday?' Perhaps he thought I'd take a pot shot at him and then maybe try to re-start WWII right there in Wincanton! Anyway he wouldn't give me his gun. But I kept on at him and tried to reassure him that I wouldn't shoot him after all why would I want to kill him and how was I supposed to get away with doing that. After a lot of pleading and some help from other folk who knew me and told him that I was OK, he agreed to let me use his shotgun. It had one barrel and he gave me one cartridge. I noticed that he left me in a bit of a hurry; I reckon he was just making sure that he was out of range. So I had one cartridge and therefore only one chance to shoot a rabbit. I aimed at the middle of the mass of rabbits in the field and fired the gun. As the shot rang out birds took to the skies in fright and the rabbits ran in all directions; well all, that is, except eleven of them. Yes with one cartridge full of lead shot I had managed to hit eleven rabbits. I went around picking them up. Some I had to knock on their heads to finish them off. Then I took the bundle of rabbits and the gun and went looking for the farmer. He couldn't believe his eyes! I never had any bother with borrowing shot guns after that and I promise I never shot any Englishmen in Wincanton!

Word got around the area that I had been a Stuka pilot in the war. I was often asked to tell stories about my sorties and particularly about being shot down behind the Russian lines. They always enjoyed that one. One day I was contacted by some aircraft enthusiasts from Bournemouth. They had got their hands on a Stuka plane and had it at Hurn Aerodrome. They wanted to know about my experiences in the Luftwaffe and were particularly keen to find out more about the Stuka. I was happy to tell them of my experiences and what it was like to fly it in combat. They wanted me to come down to Hurn with them and help them get their plane flying. It wasn't hard to persuade me. They picked me up on my day off and took me there. When we arrived I saw that sure enough it was a Junkers Stuka dive bomber. Somehow this German fighter plane was in Bournemouth. Maybe it had been dive bombing shipping in the English Channel and had been forced to land in England. I'm not sure. I was told that they had been trying to get it back into working order but that nobody at the air field had ever flown one; had I? I immediately told them that I had and so it was agreed that I should see if I could get it airborne. I was certainly ready to give it a go and climbed into the cockpit. It was the first time I had been in a pilot's seat since I had been shot down in the war. It was quite an exhilarating feeling and I wanted to get her up. It wasn't difficult to understand why British pilots would be reluctant to take her up. Stukas were quite unlike anything they were used to; an acquired taste one could say. So I went through the drill as I had on so many occasions in the war. It was almost automatic with me. But she wouldn't start. Try as we might none of us could get the engine going. So that was that. What a missed opportunity to get up in the air with my 'old friend' the Stuka again; and I've never sat in a pilot's seat in a plane since that day. It makes me sad really, mind you I'm a bit passed being a pilot at my time of life!

Walter in 2010 with his model Junkers 87 Stuka

Chapter 9
Matters of the Heart

I got to know a couple of German blokes from a nearby farm. They told me that the farmer there needed another farmhand so, with the permission of my farmer I moved there; it wasn't far away. My new job was milking all the cows. Not long after that one of those German farm workers moved to a farm in a place called Street, in Somerset. The farm was in Cranhill Road. There's no farm there these days. I went along and the farmer asked me to come and work for him, so I moved again. While I was there I got to know a chap called Mr Foisey who used to fetch the milk from the farm for his milk round. He told me about a young German woman called Hildegard he knew of and who lived nearby. He must have been a bit of a match-maker, come to think of it, trying to bring the German boy and girl together! Anyway, I was at the cinema in Street with my German friend who worked in Meare one day, and I told him about Hilde. At the time I lived next door to the farm in Cranhill Road with a family whose name I've forgotten. I went home and there she was! I was very surprised and quite excited. After we had spent some time together I walked her home. She lived near Ashcott at Huckhams Farm on Berhill, quite near the Pipers Inn. She did housework and farm work for Christopher Morland for a few shillings a week. Anyway I took her inside and we talked away, in German of course, for quite some time. I found out that she was 21 years old (I was 23 then) and that she came from Kielheim near Ragensburg. So she was Bavarian like me. She said that she had come to

England to learn to speak English and also to get away from her mother who was a bit of a witch by all accounts. Actually I met her mother once and she did look exactly like a witch, maybe she really was one! I also found out quite quickly that Hilde suffered from terrible back pains. She used to sleep with nettles in her bed every night. The nettle stings were like a drug that eased the pain so she could get through the following day. Mr Morland heard all this chatter and didn't like it. He shouted at me and told me to clear off: "Get on we don't want you here," he shouted at me. Next day he sacked Hilde - just for seeing me that one time. Hilde managed to get another job in a pub near Bridgwater but I kept my eyes open for a better job for her nearer to me. Eventually I heard that a doctor in Street needed someone to do the housework. She managed to get that job and moved back to Street, living in the doctor's house. The doctor took pity on her for the back pain that she suffered and arranged for her to have surgery in Bridgwater hospital. By this time Hilde and I had become sweethearts.

Hildegard's Story
A Conversation with Hildegard Schnitzer - April 2017

When Hildegard was just one and a half years old, she and her brother were put into an orphanage by their mother. The orphanage, or Home as sometimes referred to by Hildegard, was run in a very strict way by the Mother Superior. Although they lived in the same town as their mother - she never came to see them. By the age of six, Hildegard was taken to school by the Mother Superior. Occasionally, they would receive a message from their mother saying she was coming to see them but she never did. Not at Christmas, Easter, Birthdays or any other time.

Life at the Home was very hard at that time. There were around ten children living there. The remainder were old people. Though so young, Hildegard and the children were expected to get up at 5am every morning to ring the church bells, before attending church at 6am. There was a bowl of water left outside their dormitory door for their morning ablutions. It was so cold in the Winter the water froze solid. On mornings like this the cold forced the children to leave without making their beds properly - but on return they had to do this before they were allowed any breakfast.

Daily chores were done by the children and they also had to wash up each day after lunch at 12pm. Hildegard was so little she had to stand on a stool to reach the sink! She remembers this clearly as life at the home was so hard for them. There was never any rest. Tuesdays was ironing day, Thursdays was sock-mending and Fridays were the day the dining room had to be scrubbed clean. But Wednesdays were the worst of all. Hildegard remembers having to scrape the dirt from between the boards of the Parquet flooring with a razor blade, and then using the heavy floor polisher to bring up the shine..... it was punishing work for Hildegard who was only six years old. The windows were all cleaned on Saturdays and then it all began again the next week.

Some of the sewing skills Hildegard was forced to learn came in useful. At 10 years old she was taught to make shoes from material and she remembers making a pair of high-heeled shoes from fabric, which she wore for a long time.

Years passed and the day Hildegard left the Home and went to work, her mother came and collected a suitcase of her only belongings, which was given to her by the Mother Superior. Hildegard never saw her things again and later found out her mother had sold everything to buy cigarettes. Hildegard worked as a domestic for a year and then got a job at a Doctor's surgery helping out with all sorts of tasks including sterilisation of the instruments. She liked this job, she said.

Around this time Germany had an influx of American G.I.s and Hildegard recalled that jobs became scarce for local people as shops were plundered by these Americans. She was living with her Mother at the time - not out of choice but there was nowhere else for her to go. Hildegard had to take in washing and ironing for the Americans. They had little food and no shoes or socks. She had to go to the horsemeat market every morning at 5am and see if she could find something to take home. She often waited hours to be told they had nothing left. As recalled earlier in this book, Hildegard often had to go away for days, on her bicycle, sleeping in old abondoned buildings in her search for food. She had to disguise herself to look unattractive as the American G.I's often rampaged villages and committed tens of thousands of rapes, of the young and the old. Hildegard was only fourteen at this time. Not only did she face the danger of being found and raped, but if she dared to come home without food she faced terrible treatment by her mother. On one such occasion, having waited until ten o'clock at night at the meat market, she arrived home to be hit by her Mother for failing to get meat, and was thrown to the floor and kicked by her brother - who stood on her back with his boots - causing lifelong back injuries. Life for Hildegard was full of hardship and cruelty. Things were so bad she threatened to go with an american soldier and have a baby - just to try and get even with her Mother.   In fact Hildegard did meet an American GI by whom she became pregnant. He promised to marry her but disappeared at the end of the war back to the States. Her mother tried to force her to take pills to get rid of the baby but Hildegard flushed them down the toilet. Hildegard was also forced to chop wood from huge logs about 3 metres long. It was back breaking. She remembers well during that time that the dogs got meat to eat but she was given only black bread and water.

Kindness came from the Black American G.I.s who gave them food. They fed Hildegard and probably saved her from starvation. People's stomachs, Hildegard remembers, were swollen from hunger, while White American soldiers threw food onto the road - eggs and flour were destroyed by them rather than give them to the German people. On top of all of this, Hildegard's mother was continually nasty towards her and out of spite one day she cut her plaits off, leaving her with short hair. Meanwhile her brother was in the German Army and was shot in the lung.

Moving forward in years to Hildegard's life in England - of her life here and of Walter, Hildegard said "I only ever found happiness in England with my husband. He was too good." She has lovely memories of her life here - Working at Millfield school and cooking for 73 boys is one of them. She also remembers many kindnesses shown to Walter and her during their sixty years of marriage. She recalled the time just after they were married and moved into a very small house. They couldn't move in the kitchen, which was tiny. "We were given a wireless radio by a friend and we stood listening to it all day - it was wonderful."

Hildegard's courage was called upon on occasion during her life in England too. One time, while she worked on Morlands Farm, the Bull enclosure needed mucking out. Nobody else, including the men, would risk going into the enclosure. To everybody's surprise Hildegard went straight in and cleaned it out and put some nice bedding in there for him. She thought nothing of it. She came to the conclusion the bull was ok with her because she showed it some care and kindness, unlike the others. This is a woman who used to lie on nettles in her bed in order to numb the pain in her back. The stinging helped like an anasthetic! She also wore a plaster across her injured back for 18 years. During her pregnancy with their Son Julian, she had to go on her motorbike every

month to Bridgwater hospital to have the plaster changed as she was getting bigger! While pregnant Hildegard used to help with chopping the wood that was given to them by a friend who owned an orchard. One time while stacking the wood in their shed at home a tin of creosote spilled over her and gave her bad skin burns. Having had such a difficult upbringing, Hildegard took all this in her stride.

These days Hildgard still lives in Street and still gets up very early in the morning - sometimes as early as 4am. She continues to do beautiful and intricate cross-stitch, with which she is surrounded in her lovely home. I have included photographs of just a fraction of these wonderful pieces. Of Walter, or 'Pappa' as she tearfully and affectionately calls him "I miss him terribly. Every night I cry."

When I asked her to sum up Walter for me, she said "He was very kind to everyone. He was always giving to people. Walnuts, blackberries....We both would always rather give to people than take." And with that, in true form, Hildegard gave me a big warm hug and a beautiful cross-stitch Easter card which she had just finished. We have a quote from Walter when asked about his relationship with Hildegard. He said "We have never had an argument; she thinks the world of me and I think the world of her."

With gratitude to Hildgard for sharing her incredible story of survival and her heartfelt memories of her life with Walter. By Antoinette Ni Bhraonain

Hildegard with John Coles, author of the Foreword of this book

*Some of Hildegard's incredible
stitch work*

H.SCHNITZER 1997

PART THREE
A Working Couple

Not long after Hildegard had met and fallen in love with Walter she was admitted to Bridgwater hospital for treatment for her spine condition. When she came out of hospital she was unable to work so the regulations in place at the time meant that people in her position were not allowed to stay in Britain if they didn't have work. She would have to return to Germany even though she didn't want to go back. It was almost like Walter's situation all over again; she had nothing to go back to except a mother who hated her. So Walter said "I want you to stay here with me, let's get married then you will be allowed to stay in England". Walter continues the story........

So we decided to get married. The wedding was in the Catholic Church in Glastonbury. There were only a few guests at our wedding and nobody came from either of our families. The priest arranged a Best Man for me. I'd never met him before the day of the ceremony. Another guest was a German woman from Berlin who had married an Englishman, Mr Cousins. After the wedding there was no time or money for a honeymoon. I went home, got changed and went out to work on the farm because it was hay making time. We had very little money saved: just £18. We spent £8 on the wedding meal and the rest on a bedroom suite of furniture. At about that time I got a new job at the Avalon Leather board factory in Street.

This was part of Clarks, the shoe manufacturer's, set up. I was working on the machines that produced the material for shoe inner soles for £4/10 shillings a week, a bit better pay than farm work and I preferred the work there; I'd had enough of farm work by then. Hilde and I rented two rooms in a house in Brooks Road and a bit later on a terraced house in The Mead in Street. The rent was £5 a week. My pay didn't cover the rent so I did a hell of a lot of overtime in order to get some money together. I worked seven days a week and even got a second job for 3 hours a day on a farm out on the Meare road. Hilde also got a new job this time in the Morlands sheepskin factory in Glastonbury. She was on better money than me and with overtime took home about £20 a week. We'd done it! We'd both come to England with nothing - almost refugees. And now we were living like a proper English married couple. It felt good, but I wasn't going to stop there. I had big plans and both Hilde and I were happy to work hard to make something of our lives including owning our own home one day. One 'fly in the ointment' was our next door neighbours who were anti-German. More about that later on.

In my mid twenties I had to have an operation in the

Bristol Infirmary as I had developed a stomach ulcer. This was probably as a result of eating too many grapes and figs during my time in Italy in the war. After the operation I spent a week in a convalescent home in Bournemouth. While I was there I became friendly with an Austrian couple who were staying in the area. They actually lived in Weybridge in Surrey and had bought a mobile home to live in. T hat was becoming quite a popular housing option in those days of housing shortages. I told them about the trouble we were having with our neighbours and they suggested that we buy our own mobile home and move to live near them. So Hilde and I went to see their home and we thought it was a good idea for us. We could have our very own home at a price we could afford. So we did just that. We bought a mobile home near theirs and then just paid rent for the plot.

We both had to find new jobs of course. I found work at a plywood factory in Weybridge and Hildegard got a job in a tobacconist and sweet shop. lt was lovely to have our own home and of course we had escaped from the nasty neighbours. But Hilde didn't like living in Weybridge . Actually we both missed

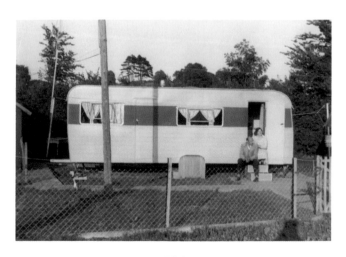

Somerset and all the friends we had made down there. So after about nine months we moved back. We wanted to keep our mobile home and we found a place for it in Pedwell. But we needed to move our mobile home down to there. I asked around and found a bloke who had a Yanky Jeep who said he could tow it for me. Now normally you have to put mobile homes onto a low loader to move them. After all they are much longer (ours was 22 feet long) and wider than touring caravans and the wheels are not designed for more than moving short distances. There aren't even any proper brakes or road lights. Well he just hitched it up to his Jeep and towed it all the way. The police never stopped him. I followed on my motor bike and Hilde managed to ride all that way on her little NSU Quickly moped! When we had the mobile home in position I asked the bloke who had towed it down how much I owed him - £5, he said- I couldn't believe it! Being back in Somerset felt very good and we both got our old jobs back, me at Avalon Leather Board Factory and Hilde at Morlands Sheepskin Factory.

I mention my motor bike. In the early days in England I had a push bike but as our savings built up I was able to afford motorized transport. My first bike was an Ariel Square 4 with a sidecar which cost me £250 second hand. That was a hefty sum in those days, probably about six months pay for me. Actually that bike gave me nothing but trouble so I sold it after about 6 months and bought a brand new Triumph Thunderbird 600cc with a sidecar. T hat's when Hildegard bought her NSU Quickly moped. We were a two-bike family! And we could both get about to our places of work and go off together on my machine when we wanted to. I had a succession of Triumph Thunderbird bikes. One with a German bullet-style sidecar. I bought my last motorbike in 1951 and also got a pickup van. Much later in 1973 I bought my first really decent German car. A brand new Audi 100 which cost me £999 - a fortune then! It was a dream car.

Next to our mobile home park in Pedwell was a farm. I asked the farmer if he could give me some part-time work. So even though I had a full time job and did overtime at the Avalon Leather Board factory and also worked part-time at Cradlebridge farm near Glastonbury, just behind Snows Timber Yard. I now had a third job! I tell you I've never been afraid of work. At the farm in Pedwell I did lots of farm work, like milking and cutting kale, but the thing I remember most, probably because I still have a photo, was when I had to cut down all the elm trees at the farm. This was because Dutch Elm Disease was killing trees all over the country. When I had cut down the trees I sawed and chopped them up into logs for the stove in our mobile home. It was a massive job. Maybe you have seen pictures of Bavarian houses with huge roofs and large over-hanging eaves with stacks of logs piled up under them ready for winter fires. Well what Hilde and I made was the biggest pile of logs you ever saw. It was twice the height of a person and about 12 feet long and 3 feet wide.

A Baby

Julian was born in 1964 while we lived in Pedwell. In 1967 Hildegard and I made our first fisit back to Bavaria. Julian was just three years old. I went ot see some of my family. First we went to Munich to see Eddi who I had kept in touch with. He took me to meet some toher members of my family including Otto. Eddi said to Otto: "Who do you think this is then?" He didn't recognise me!

Family life with Walter and Hildegard

Walter and Hildegard st their Pedwell Caravan shortly after they were married

Above: A photograph of Hildegard taken in the mid-1960s, Hildegard always enjoyed gardening

Above: Walter and Hildegard's son Julian and their four granddaughters pictured in 1997

The Grandchildren Kirsty, Emma, Samantha and Sophia pictured here in 2006

Above: Walter and
Hildegard with Julian
and family in 2009

In later years Walter and Hildegard travelled
back to Bavaria several times on holidays

The Luftwaffe pilot who found love and a home in Somerset

Walter Schnitzer and wife Hildegard pictured celebrating 60 years of marriage in 2011, main picture; Councillor John Coles, above left; and fighting during the Battle of Stalingrad

113

Anglo-German relations

I like England and the English people. I've never been interested in politics, or religion for that matter. I've always been too busy getting on with my life and earning a living to be bothered with all that. Have you heard about the German work ethic? It really is true what they say about us. We Germans, well most of us anyway, are not afraid of hard work. Even before I arrived in England I was never involved in all the mass hysteria that happened with Hitler and the Nazis. I didn't even join the Hitler Youth although I was supposed to. I wasn't interested. I'm just an ordinary bloke who happened to be born in Germany. But after the war finished and I was no longer a POW I came across quite a few English people who were prejudiced against Germans and gave me a hard time. Now you might think that's understandable and that they were the generation of English people who had suffered in the war; those whose houses were bombed or ones who lost loved ones in the fighting in the war. Actually it wasn't any of them. The ones who called me names and did nasty things to me were people who hadn't actually been directly involved in the war. Like our neighbours in The Mead for instance who were always unpleasant to Hilde and me just because we're German. That family actually put live fireworks through our window! The police weren't very helpful and the abuse carried on. That's why we decided to move away from there. I had a great working relationship with my colleagues at the leather Board factory. Only one bloke gave me any grief. It was in about 1953, a few years after the war had ended. He called me a Nazi and spat in my face. I just came right back and hit him hard across his face.

He never made a complaint and nothing was ever said about the incident. And he never tried that on me again. That was the only incident like that in the 38 years that I worked there.

The war ended a long time ago as you know but sadly some people just can't forget about it. Maybe it's the media's fault. Even children's comics these days have war stories in them - why? A few weeks ago when I was out on my disability 'buggy' wearing my Bavarian hat and coat as I always do, a bloke came over to me and said: "You're going to kill someone on that thing. Why don't you take it over to your country and kill a few of 'em over there instead!" Why did he have to say that? And would an Englishman living in Germany ever have to put up with that sort of thing? I don't think so. I remember being taught at school that we should never hate people from other countries. I know that war can bring out the worst in human beings but that happens on all sides I think. And the war ended a long time ago! I think it's a shame that people like that are so small-minded and prejudiced. We are all really the same; we're all human beings living together on this planet trying to make the best of things. These incidents are upsetting and I do remember them but like I said there were only a few bad moments in all those years.

Junkers Ju 87 Stuka

If ever there was to be an effective weapon that could be termed as being successful as well as deadly, it would have to be the Junkers Ju87, known to Germans as the Sturzkampfbomber, and better known to the English as a dive bomber or better still a "Stuka". No other aircraft can make claim to the number of ships sunk and also it ranks second to the number of enemy tanks destroyed during times of warfare.

The Junkers Ju87 was an attacking aircraft. Normally carrying one 250 kg bomb (later 500 kg) under the fuselage and up to four 50kg bombs under the wings, a formation of Ju87 "Stuka" dive bombers became a deadly cocktail, flying directly overhead of their target, then dive bombing at an angle of almost 90 degrees. During the campaigns in Spain, Poland and the Low Countries, these deadly formations were devastating. But over the English Channel during the Battle of Britain, they could not compete against the superior Hurricane and Spitfire and they ceased to become the attacking force that they were so well known for, and became the victims themselves.

Although a technique of dive bombing existed during the First World War, there was no aircraft designed primarily for this purpose. The first known aircraft designed for the purpose of dive bombing was the Junkers K47 which was being developed during the mid 1920's, and which flew for the first time in March 1928. It is believed that of the fourteen built, two remained in Germany while twelve were sold to China. Continuing research showed that such aircraft would be an effective weapon when working in close support of ground forces. Advances would be far more effective if concentrated aerial bombardment could pave the way for mechanized troops and infantry and Germany made the decision to manufacture aircraft suited for this role. In 1933, Henschel developed the Hs123 while Junkers continued development of the K47.

Where the Hs123 was a biplane, the Ju87, developed from the K47 was a single engined monoplane that differed from all previous Junkers aircraft in that it did not have the corrugated ribbed metal stressed skin appearance. Looking very similar to the "Stuka" of the 1940's, the prototype had a fixed undercarriage and the gull-wing appearance and was powered by a Rolls-Royce Kestrel power plant, and made its first flight in May 1935. Full scale production of the aircraft commenced in 1937. The first variant was the Ju87A- 1 and had dive brakes added to the outer wings, the kestrel engine was replaced by a Jumo 210Ca 640 horsepower engine which drove a variable pitch three bladed propeller, and a single tail fin replaced the twin fins of the original design. The Ju87A-1 and Ju87A-2 (The A-2 differed by having larger fairings over the landing gear and having a 680 hp Jumo 210Da engine) was delivered to StG163 which saw action with the legion Condor in Spain and the Gruppen proved very effective. By early 1939, all the A series were sent to training units and all the Stukageschwader were equipped with the more powerful Ju87B series. These were powered by the Jumo 211A direct injection power plant that produced 1,200hp, had more streamlined spats over the landing gear, and was now equipped with an automatic dive control.

This automatic dive control was an apparatus that was initially set by the pilot, allowing him to choose the pull out height using a contact altimeter. The whole procedure became necessary for the pilot to go through about ten different actions with the apparatus before he opened up the dive brakes under the outer wings. This automatically commenced the dive action of the aircraft, the pilot adjusting the dive angle manually by indicator lines painted on the canopy of the aircraft. the correct line was achieved by aileron control which was usually at about 90 degrees, and the pilot visually seeing his target by the marker on the canopy. With the aircraft hurtling earthwards directly at the target, a signal light on the contact altimeter would then come on and the pilot would press the button on the top of his control column and the pull out would commence as the bombs left their cradles. The bombs would continue the same course as the aircraft had during its dive, towards the target while the pilot would be suffering some 6g as the aircraft levelled out ready for its climb skywards.

The accuracy of the bombing run was completely in the hands of the pilot. Its defence were two MG81 belt fed machine guns. The rear gunner operated a machine gun which was reasonably effective, but it was the slow top speed of the aircraft and the poor rate of climb that was to be the downfall of the Ju87. Over combat areas of Europe and in Spain, they managed to hold their own, but they were no match for the fast and manoeuvrable Hurricanes and Spitfires of the RAF. Whole Gruppen were being destroyed on missions over the English Channel, and the Luftwaffe had no alternative but to withdraw them from operation duties during this period, although as the war progressed, further variants were produced and the Ju87 saw service in Europe and in the Mediterranean.

Junkers Ju 878 Stuka Specifications

Ju 87 G-2, Werk Nr. 494083 preserved in 1970 wearing code W8-A. Maintained by RAF St Athan, displayed at RAF Chivenor.}} |Source ={{own}} |Author =RuthAS |Date =22 August 1970...

Type	Anti-Tank Aircraft/Anti-Shipping Strike Aircraft
Power Plant	Junkers Jumo 211 Da 1,400hp
Unladen weight	9,700lbs (4400Kg)
Laden weight	14,550lbs (6600Kg)

Max Speed	Approx 195 mph (314 kph)
Cruising Speed	Approx 118 mph (190 kph)
Rate of Climb	Not known
Max range	199 miles (320 kms)
Service Ceiling	Not known
Armament	2 x fixed MG81 machine guns
	+ 1 removable MG81
Wingspan	49ft 2 ½ (15m)
Length	37ft 8 3/4 (11.50m)

Junkers Ju-87 "Stuka "

The Stuka was the most famous of all planes used by the Germans as a sturzkamflugzeug (dive bomber). The Stuka was designed strictly as an army co-operation dive bomber at the urging of General Emst Udet. It is instantly recognisable with its inverted gull-wings, and fixed undercarriage. The Ju-87 was ugly, sturdy, accurate, but very vulnerable to enemy fighters. The Germans learned in the Battle of Britain that its use demanded air superiority. It was too slow, unmanoeuvrable and under-armed, but its effectiveness in destroying vehicles, fortifications or ships, or just scaring people, was undoubted. Its accuracy was high when in a full dive that was up to 80 degrees. Once the bomb was released it used an automatic pull-up system to ensure that the plane pulled out of the dive even if the pilot blacked out from the high G-forces. The Germans fitted the wheel covers with sirens that were used once the planes went into a dive to shatter the morale of enemy troops and civilians. They also fitted whistles onto the fins of the bombs to ensure that the recipients knew just when the bombs were released and could track them on the way down. Over 5,700 Stukas were built.

The Ju 87B-1 flew with a crew of 2, the pilot and a rear-gunner. The engine was an 880kW Junkers Jumo 211Da that could pull the aircraft up to 385km/h. It had an operational ceiling of 8000m and a range of only 600km. Its armament was three 7.9mm machine guns and either one 500kg bomb or four 50 kg bombs fitted to racks either under the fuselage or under the inboard portion of the wings.

From 1942 on the Ju 87G-1 was a dedicated anti-tank aircraft on the eastern front. It was fitted with a 1400hp Junkers Jumo 211 J engine. It had a maximum speed of 314km/h, a ceiling of 8000m and a very limited range of only 320km. The reduced speed and range was due to the armour plating installed to protect the pilot and gunner when flying low-level tank busting missions. It was armed with two 30mm cannons in pods under the wings and a 7.92mm machine gun in the back for the gunner.